TO KEEP THEM ALIVE

SALLY TONGREN

TO KEEP THEM ALIVE

ALIVE

WILD ANIMAL BREEDING

DEMBNER BOOKS · NEW YORK

Dembner Books

Published by Red Dembner Enterprises Corp., 80 Eighth Avenue, New York, N.Y. 10011

Distributed by W. W. Norton & Company, Inc., 500 Fifth Avenue, New York, N.Y. 10110

Library of Congress Cataloging in Publication Data

Tongren, Sally.
    To keep them alive.

    Includes index.
    1. Zoo animals—Breeding.   2. Wild animals, Captive—
Breeding.   I. Title.
SF408.3.T66   1985   636.08′2   85-4599
ISBN 0-934878-66-8

Acknowledgments

The story of captive propagation is not just the story of one zoo. Many fine institutions all over the world are engaged in this effort, and it would be possible to illustrate the triumphs and frustrations of animal breeding from the work of any one of these. But the zoo that I know best is the National Zoological Park in Washington, D.C., and therefore, I have drawn heavily, although not exclusively, upon this zoo's experience.

While much of the information in this book comes from professional books and journals, it is also derived from my thirteen years of experience as a volunteer guide at the Zoo. During those years, and still today, I have had the satisfaction of sharing the excitement that I find in animals with many school children and a goodly number of adults as I have introduced them to the Zoo's animal inhabitants. Over the years I have had wonderful opportunities to see some of the inner workings of the Zoo and to gain an appreciation of the important work that is going on there. The Zoo Staff have been more than generous in granting me interviews and answering my questions. I hasten to add, however, that nothing I say here should be taken as official policy of the National Zoo. The achievements are theirs: the errors and omissions are all my own.

I would like to extend my thanks to the following people at the National Zoo for furnishing me with information or materials and for reviewing all or part of this manuscript. Jonathan Ballou, Judith Block, Elizabeth Frank, Dr. Jo Gayle Howard, Dr. Edwin Gould, Dr. Dale Marcellini, Robert Mulcahy, Dr. Olav Oftedal, Charles Pickett, Miles Roberts, Judith White, William Xanten. My friends of the Friends of the National Zoo staff and my fellow volunteers have been generous with anecdotes and sympathy. I thank Dr. Theodore Reed, the former Director, for allowing me to roam about the zoo collecting information, and Dr. Michael Robinson, the present Director, for supporting that decision, and both of them for reading the result. Photographer Jessie Cohen of the Office of Graphics and Exhibits has made an essential contribution with her fine photographs as has photographer Milton Tierney. Dr. Devra Kleiman gave me great assistance with information and comments on the work in progress as well as by reviewing the final product. I feel a special gratitude to Dr. Robert Hoage for his interest, patience, and encouragement.

CONTENTS

FOREWORD

The world is so full of a number of things,
I'm sure we all should be happy as kings.
A Child's Garden of Verses

When we who are now reaching our middle years first read these words by Robert Louis Stevenson, we may not have been as happy as kings, but we were indeed the heirs of a world full of a number of things. Among them was a multitude of wild places—torrid jungles, misty tundra, silent mountains valleys—about which we could sit and dream, and, in our mind's eye, conjure up their inhabitants. Whether our fancies took the form of glowing tigers or ponderous rhinos, moustachioed walruses or soaring condors, we knew that those animals were out there somewhere, ours if only for the dreaming then, but creatures that we might someday meet face to face.

Our grandchildren are not likely to be so fortunate. They may dream their dreams, but these are unlikely to be based in reality. The creatures of their dreams might very well be what the dinosaurs are to us, things of the past, creatures of fantasy. Today several hundred species of large animals, and probably thousands of very small ones, are threatened with extinction, about to join the dodo and the dinosaur, unless someone does something to prevent this.

Some of these creatures are so familiar, so much a part of our world view that it seems inconceivable that they should ever disappear. They are imbedded in our history and our culture. They teach us our letters, they march in solemn procession into Noah's Ark, they figure in folk song and fable. These birds and beasts appear in the great art of many civilizations, from the caves of Altamira to the present; our imagery and our language would be empty without them.

The wilds would be empty. Which of us can imagine the warm African dawn without a rhino ambling back to its wallow after a night of browsing; or a South American forest that no longer adds its shadow pattern to the jaguar's spotted coat; or our own spring woodlands without the waves of migrating warblers?

The wilds themselves are vanishing, and herein lies the major reason for these animal's threatened status. It is true that there are other pressures upon them. The spotted cats have been hunted down for their fur; elephants for their ivory. The tiger and the rhinoceros have been sought as walking pharmacopoeias, bearing on four feet cures for human ills and egos. Elephants and tigers, wolves and lions have been perceived— and sometimes with reason—as a threat to human interests. All of these factors have acted to reduce the numbers of these particular species, but today the greatest threat to wild animals, as a whole, comes from the expanding human populations, whose needs for land are leading to a massive clearing of forests, draining of marshes, and plowing of savannahs. Habitat destruction cuts across all species of animals and plants, threatening the existence of many that would otherwise live undisturbed. In a world where human population is increasing exponentially, and, with it, the human need for enough land to eke out a bare existence, a great many wonderful creatures are likely to be simply crowded off the face of the earth.

Human needs must be served. Hungry children must be fed and people all over the world have a right to a more secure economic future. No one can argue with this. But much forest clearing offers little immediate benefit, and even less long-term benefit to the landless. The tremendous diversity of the tropical forest may be replaced by small farms, but more often it is replaced by sugar plantations and coffee plantations, or by cattle pastures that furnish beef to fast-food chains in the United States. The peasant may find employment on one of these, but the steady flow of people into Mexico City or Rio De Janeiro or Nairobi suggests that this is not always true.

Even opening land to farmers is not always successful, and well-intentioned projects may have unforeseen effects. Brazilian planners who have opened a new frontier to homesteaders have found that in many areas the tropical soils lose their fertility within a year or so, and can only be farmed by the addition of expensive and imported fertilizers, and sometimes not even then. In 1969, 22,000 acres of the Volcanos National Park in Rwanda, the last refuge of the mountain gorilla, were cleared and planted with pyrethrum (used as an insecticide), intended for export in an attempt to improve that nation's fragile economy. Forests act as vast sponges, however, holding rains and slowly releasing water into the lands below, and the loss of these forests resulted in a forty per cent reduction of the stream flow in the bottom lands, where farmers relied on this water in the dry season. The world is a complex mechanism.

If this book seems to be a tale of the tropics, that does not imply that there are no problems elsewhere. We have many here in the United States, and with our record of exterminating, in a few years, the passenger pigeon (which once comprised one of the

In the United States we have recently reached a tenuous balance with timber wolves and other members of our native fauna.

vastest bird populations the world had ever seen) and nearly wiping out the bison, one of the greatest mammal aggregations, we are hardly in a position to assume a pious attitude. If we have, in the last ten years, attained a tenuous balance with our remaining wildlife, that does not give us the right to criticize the new nations for their shortcomings in wildlife management. Rather it behooves us to offer our help and cooperation in an effort that is of importance to us all.

Without laying blame, the greatest wildlife crises today do lie in the tropical nations, especially in the tropical forests—the location of the greatest diversity of life on this planet. Cose to seventy percent of the world's species of plants and animals are native to tropical forests—not seventy per cent of all plants and animals, but seventy per cent of the different *kinds* of plants and animals. This includes animals in the broadest sense, from earthworms to elephants, boa constrictors to bowerbirds. If these creatures seem remote from our concerns, it is well to remember that among these species are the migratory birds that breed among us and brighten our summer woodlands, but that winter in those tropical forests. "Our" birds are also "their" birds and the number of birds that return to the breeding grounds will be determined by the fate of the wintering grounds.

Today, tropical lands are being cleared, converted to farms, pastures, and plantations—when they are not becoming eroded deserts—at a rate that is unprecedented in human history. In the *Global 2000 Report to the President,* Dr. Thomas Lovejoy of the World Wildlife Fund estimates that by the year 2000 about two-thirds of the existing tropical forests will have been cleared. That is two-thirds of the forests that exist today. Half of the original African forest is gone already, forty per cent of the Southeast Asian forests, about a quarter of the South American ones. Lovejoy projects that when these forests are cleared, about one-eighth of the world's species of plants and animals will have become extinct, some before we have even identified them.

Changes in land use already have progressed to the point where much of our tropical wildlife is restricted to national parks and various game and biological reserves. (In fact, much of *all* wildlife, worldwide, is so restricted.) By the year 2000, if present trends continue, these reserves, along with a few other scraps of native vegetation too poor or inaccessible to be worth clearing, will stand alone as little islands in a sea of farms and plantations. While a lucky few species of plants and animals may find one of these parks as an island of refuge, those that are unlucky will in all probability become extinct and vanish from our world for all time.

This situation will not go away. Population growth among tropical countries is exploding. Rwanda is the second most densely populated nation in the world; Kenya's population will reach sixty million by 2000; similar projections can be found for most African and South American nations. There are a great many people in the world and only so much land, and even if every nation in the world limited families to one or two children, as have the Chinese, this rate of growth would still be with us. In these nations, half or more of the population may be under fifteen and yet to bear their own families, while the life expectancy of their elders has increased appreciably.

There are no simple solutions, but many individuals, organizations, and governments are working today to save as much of the planet's diversity of plant and animal life as possible. The first line of defense lies in the parks and reserves which form part of the essential habitats of these creatures. It is important to establish as many of these as possbile, to make them as large as possible—to attempt to include a substantial part of a complete ecosystem. It will be important to establish buffer zones between park and farm and, ideally, to link areas of reserve by corridors where animals may travel in safety. Many reserves will fall short of this, but they will still serve a valuable purpose.

Many of the tropical nations already have good park systems—some are admirable—that are served by dedicated men and women, but they have the problems of their rapidly growing populations and weak economies. These limit the amount of land that can be set aside and the degree of security that can be guaranteed. Warfare and rebellions are no respecters of park boundaries. Parks are political creations, and what can be established by government action can be disestablished in the same way. In spite of efforts to teach those who live on a park's boundaries about its value to the nation, it is all too easy for poverty-stricken people to see a reserve as something that has no relation to their lives except to take up land on which they might be able to raise food.

Differences in perception may arise from poverty, or they may reflect different priorities and traditions. We see this in the United States when those to whom the wilderness means solitude and silence come into conflict with those to whom a snowy road calls for a snowmobile, or a mountain lake for water skis. These differences may be even more pronounced in a nation without a long conservation tradition.

The La Macarena National Park in Colombia is an isolated mountain that biologists consider extremely important to that nation's efforts to preserve its wildlife. While it was being established as a park, border stations were built and trails cleared to give access to the interior for surveys. In the surrounding area were a number of people who had been driven out of the mountains to the west by civil strife some years before. They simply flowed back into the park along the new trails, bypassing guards who had no stake in the preservation of the park and probably held the same view of its value as the local people. The government, realizing that the reserve could not be maintained as a park with people living in it, lopped off the section that had been settled, only to have the settlers move farther in as new trails were cut.

Zoologist Robert Cooper, who worked with the Peace Corps in Colombia at that time, commented: "There are cultural reasons why things cannot be guarded as well as economic reasons. . . . [Establishing the reserve] is the best example of a sincere effort on the part of many people, and a rather rare one, and yet these efforts at preservation in my estimation have had more to do with allowing the colonists to come in than anything, and the future promises to be the same. That which will be protected is that which is most inaccessible, that which is most inhospitable."

Another serious question in the minds of biologists is whether the reserves will be large enough to support healthy populations of some species over a long period of time. Even the largest national parks in the United States do not include enough land to preserve the mountain lion or the grizzly bear. Scientists must therefore ponder certain questions: Will there come to be so many animals that the parks will become animal slums as their inhabitants destroy their own habitat? Will some be forced out, to become vulnerable to hunters, or to destroy herds and crops (so that they have to be killed)? Will there be enough animals for a genetically sound population? Will there be space for new generations?

In spite of all misgivings, habitat protection, whether it is by parks or national forests, game reserves, or whatever they are called, is essential. There is absolutely no valid alternative that will provide the protection needed for so wide a rang of species. A reserve for tigers or elephants or crocodiles has the side effect of protecting all sorts of animals or plants that have no press agents, and in reverse, the presence of an endangered species may protect a certain habitat. We must have reserves, but that does not mean that we must rely on that single option to protect all species.

Many biologists and conservationists are now beginning to look seriously at captive propagation as a second line of defense for species that may, for one reason or another, be especially vulnerable and thus unlikely to survive in the wild. This has always been a controversial issue in the counservation community, but today there is a growing consensus that it would be wise to establish large, healthy breeding groups of threatened species in captivity while there is still time to do it. Gerald Durrell, the noted British naturalist and writer, who by establishing the Jersey Wildlife Preservation Trust has probably done as much to promote this concept to the general public (and to his own profession) as anyone living, says, "As soon as a species is proved to be on the wane, a captive breeding program should be set up *automatically.*"

Captive breeding—taking plants and animals from the wild and raising them under controlled conditions—has been going on ever since a Stone Age hunter scooped up a wolf pup and carried it home to grow up in his cave and help him hunt. All of our

A far cry from the bars and cramped space of the old menagerie cage, a roomy modern zoo enclosure provides grass and shade for a lioness and her cub.

domestic animals and food plants had wild ancestors; today we have fox farms and mink ranches, salmon farms in Canada and Scotland, and farms in New Zealand and Scotland where red deer are raised for food.

The aim of this kind of breeding is to shape animals to human needs. Early hunters and farmers tried many animals, including an Egyptian attempt at hyena domestication, before they settled on those that were most suitable for their purposes. Once these had been chosen, they began to practice selective breeding, for although they knew nothing of genetics, they clearly saw the end result and picked the sheep with the thickest wool and the cows with the richest milk to be the parents of the next generation. Horses were bred for speed and endurance; dogs were shaped into the Great Dane and the Pekinese. Today, most of these animals bear little resemblance to the wild type and would be unlikely to survive without human care.

There are those who fear, with some basis, that captive propagation will have a similar result, yielding deer that are only cows with antlers, and tamed and shabby tigers. Today's breeders are well aware of this danger. The best managers of captive animals try to keep them as they are in the wild, not to tame or breed them to an idealized type. They try to select, as the parents of the next generation, those animals that will assure that the diversity of the wild population is preserved, and which will produce a healthy and genetically sound stock for the future. Such aims are not easy to achieve, but the intent is clear.

Zoos are the logical locations for captive propagation. Not only do they have experience and stocks of animals on hand, but they have a vested interest in the success of the project. Large or small, they offer great skill in the husbandry of exotic animals, and the larger zoos have the scientific staffs that are needed to conduct the studies that lead to better management of animals both in the zoo and in the wild.

The zoo is no longer isolated from the wild. Study of wild animals in their natural settings is essential to the proper care of captive animals, and zoologists from the zoo also work in the field. The combination of field and captive studies of animal behavior and physiology serves to improve captive breeding records and provides vital information for reserve managers. As animals are increasingly confined to small reserves, their care will pose many of the same problems that already face managers of zoo animals. During the course of field studies such scientists from the zoo often train and assist wildlife biologists of developing nations, so that the impetus for wildlife management and conservation education may come from within rather than being imposed from without.

Critics of captive propagation—and of zoos—point to historically poor breeding records in zoos. It is true that, although there have been zoos since the time of the Chou Dynasty in China in the 12th century B.C., until recently few of them concentrated on breeding. Zoos were essentially parks with animals, places of recreation that might, just possibly, be educational for young children. Most zoos tried to outdo their rivals, keeping as many kinds of animals as possible, trying to have the biggest or the oldest one in captivity. Animals were often exhibited as single specimens, which obviously made breeding impossible. Even if there was a pair their needs and habits were so unfamiliar that reproduction was largely a matter of luck. What zoo babies did appear were the offspring of animals, such as lions, that will breed under the worst of conditions; in fact, it is nearly impossible to keep them from breeding. Baby animals make wonderful exhibits, but no one worried very much when these failed to appear; it was just one of those things. Many kinds of animals were considered impossible to breed in captivity, and in any case, there were plenty more to be had from the wild. Not surprisingly, the breeding record was poor.

These practices, however, are changing rapidly. In the 1960s, the directors of the world's zoos began to realize that if they did not look to their breeding records they would soon be out of business. It was no longer possible to send out an expedition and bring back a cargo of assorted birds and beasts or call a dealer and order up a rhino or hippo. Animals had become very rare and, as a result, had become extremely

Zoo-bred animals, contributed by the New York Zoological Society, played an important part in saving the American bison from extinction.

expensive. As the 1960s progressed, it became clear that many species were not only rare but that an appalling number were rare to the point of becoming extinct.

Groups such as the American Association of Zoological Parks and Aquariums (AAZPA) and the International Union of Directors of Zoological Gardens (IUDZG) began to work together on ways in which they could become self-sufficient in exhibit animals, and thus end the drain on the wild populations. They began to regulate themselves, setting higher standards for care and agreeing not to import certain endangered species. What was once a mild interest in appealing babies has become an intense interest in self-sustaining populations of exhibit animals, and plans for well-managed cooperative programs for the preservation of endangered species are now under way. At their best, today's zoos are becoming banks where animals and the genes that they carry are kept on deposit for the benefit of future generations.

There are many complexities in breeding programs, for they must take into account not only the welfare of a tiger cub born today, but that of one born twenty or fifty years from now. This means careful planning of the physical environment. It means providing the best of food and medical care. It means carefully hatching eggs and rearing babies. It also means more complex, and heretofore unconsidered, questions of genetics and animal behavior and plans for providing homes for the growing numbers of youngsters from successful programs.

All zoos face these problems, but they may solve them in different ways. Different climates dictate different kinds of housing; different administrative systems need different sorts of records; there are differences in budgets and there are personal preferences for species and programs. As in any human endeavor, there are differences of opinion—and sometimes personal differences—but progress in cooperative programs is growing steadily.

Zoos come in different shapes and sizes. The San Diego Zoo, located in the mild southern California climate, is a wonderful garden, with many rare and beautiful plants as well as exotic animals that can spend almost all of the year outdoors. It has the largest staff of veterinarians of any zoo in the United States and correspondingly excellent care. The San Diego Zoological Society also operates the San Diego Wild Animal Park at San Pasqual, a facility with a first-rate breeding record. Here on 1,800 acres of open range visitors aboard a monorail watch giraffes and antelope and the second biggest herd of white rhinos outside Africa. The combined facilities operate on a budget of around 45 million a year.

But not all zoos are big or high priced. The Arizona–Sonora Desert Museum in Tucson, Arizona, specializes in the birds, mammals, and reptiles of its own desert area,

Captive bred birds are a hopeful sign that the wild voice of the Mississippi Sandhill Crane will still be heard.

and places a heavy emphasis on education. In this, it has the assistance of one hundred and fifty volunteers in addition to ninety employees, and operates on $2,500,000 a year. And the Salisbury Zoo, in Salisbury, Maryland, is a delightful, small municipal zoo with a well-cared-for collection that manages on about $234,000.

The Brookfield Zoo in Chicago now exhibits monkeys and apes in a building the size of a football field, where visitors walk through a rain forest, seemingly among the apes. The Minnesota Zoo also has a huge tropical house in addition to its many animals that feel at home in Minnesota winters, such as Siberian tigers, Bactrian camels, and musk oxen. The list could go on forever.

No one zoo is *the* leader in the field of captive propagation. The leaders are people and they come from many institutions. It would be possible to illustrate the problems and achievements of captive propagation from any of these. Because it is the zoo I know best, this book draws on the experience of the National Zoological Park, although not exclusively.

The National Zoo lies in the heart of Washington, D.C., a part of the 1,700 acres of Rock Creek Park. Thanks in part to its location within the park, it has a beautiful setting of large, old trees and rocky ledges and seems far removed from the bustle of the city, although sable antelope gaze out at buses passing on Connecticut Avenue and the wail of passing sirens often brings a response from the white-cheeked gibbons. It has a fine and varied collection of animals, the most famous being the two giant pandas, Ling-Ling and Hsing-Hsing.

The National Zoo is a research center as well. It is a part of the Smithsonian Institution, and was established in 1889, a time when some scientists were first beginning to fear for the future of many North American wild animals. There has always been an implied interest in conservation within the institution in addition to its mandate to operate "for the advancement of science and the instruction and recreation of the people." There may be other institutions, notably the Bronx Zoo and the New York Zoological Society, that have had a wider impact on field research, but the work of the National Zoo, combined with the work of Smithsonian scientists, must run a close second in this, and possibly lead in behavioral research on captive animals. It is unique in that its $9,265,563 operating budget comes from the federal government. Two hundred and seventy-nine employees work in the Zoo, from curators and keepers to plumbers and welders, and there are six hundred and fifty volunteers, working in a number of capacities.

The emphasis on conservation at the National Zoo has grown, leading to the establishment of the Conservation and Research Center, located on 3,000 acres of wooded hillsides and open fields near Front Royal, Virginia. This is purely a breeding farm and research station, not open to the public, but its rolling pastures provide space for herds of such rare species as Père David's deer, scimitar-horned oryx, and several species of cranes, while camels or emus standing on the skyline often startle passing motorists.

The National Zoo is blessed with a dedicated and outstanding staff, although, in fairness, many zoos seem to attract dedicated people to an extent that is far out of proportion to the monetary rewards. Like most zoos, the National Zoo can boast of successes and regret failures in breeding its animals, but even such failures as are part of its record also serve to provide information for a field that is still in its infancy, for all its long history.

It is important for those of us who feel a concern for the future of wild things to understand and be aware of what these, and other fine zoos, are doing today. Changes in their thinking will affect what we will see in zoos and in the future of many of the animals that hold our interest. We will see fewer kinds of animals in any one zoo, but more of each kind. We may have to visit several zoos before we can see the whole of Noah's Ark, for zoos are beginning to specialize. We may see more unfamiliar animals, although there will still be "lions and tigers and bears."

As laymen we have a part to play, an important one, for our support is needed to make these breeding programs possible. Our understanding of the aims of these programs and sympathy for the changes that result are essential if zoos are to fulfill their newly assumed responsibilities. These are expensive programs. William Conway, Director of the Bronx Zoo, has estimated that to keep five hundred members of each of two hundred species of animals for the next twenty years will cost about as much as it did to put a man on the moon—about twenty-five billion dollars. We as taxpayers supported the moon flights, and not only as taxpayers but as generally enthusiastic advocates and vicarious participants. Our moral and financial support, expressed through whatever contribution we can make, be it monetary contribution or lobbying effort on behalf of our local zoo, or by giving time as a volunteer or simply understanding, will go far to determine the success of this, possibly less spectacular but more altruistic project. If we do this, then perhaps our children will still be able to fill their dreams with real elephants and rhinos, giant pandas and golden lion tamarins.

BRAZILIAN GOLD

A tiny ball of golden fur nestles in his keeper's hand. Slender arms clasp her thumb trustingly, but the bright, dark eyes that gaze out from this haven look on a world that has shown little concern for the fate of small monkeys. This is a baby golden lion tamarin, one of the earth's rarest mammals. Many people consider golden lion tamarins to be the earth's most beautiful mammal, as well. They are monkeys in miniature. Even the largest of the full grown males weigh only a little over a pound and, except for their long slender tails, would fit neatly into your cupped hands. Their coats are glossy, and range in color from the ruddy gold of the proverbial new-minted penny to paler shades of white gold. Lion-like manes frame their expressive little tan faces, which account for the name of lion tamarin.

Only one hundred or so golden lion tamarins still live in their native Brazilian forests, but thanks to an intensive program of research into the complexities of tamarin social life, over four hundred now live in zoos all over the world, a deposit of living gold more valuable than anything in a Swiss bank vault.

To fully understand the golden lion tamarin story, we must step back in history, almost five hundred years. When Portuguese explorers first reached Brazil in 1501, they found the coastline around what is now Rio de Janeiro covered with a dense, moist forest inhabited by a wonderful array of birds and beasts, including golden lion tamarins. The Portuguese, then preoccupied with their East Indian ventures, were slow to colonize this new territory. In time, however, settlers came, cleared the forests, established sugar plantations, farms, and pastures, and bit by bit the coastal forest vanished; today, about two per cent of that original forest remains in remote areas. For the rest, only small clumps of forest still stand, isolated on inaccessible hilltops separated by baked, eroded fields covered with scrubby grass. For all their small size, golden lion tamarins need more space than such a landscape can offer, and as their forests have vanished so have they.

Tamarins were also captured for the pet trade and, to a lesser degree, for exhibition in zoos and use as laboratory animals, a practice that cost the lives of far more animals

Golden lion tamarins, miniature monkeys in silky golden coats, are considered by many to be among the most beautiful of mammals.

than ever reached their new destinations. In reality, tamarins do not make very satisfactory pets; they are delicate, demanding, and inclined to nip fingers, but their beauty and beguiling ways created a market even in the 17th and 18th centuries. Bearing witness to this trade, a golden lion tamarin peers at us from a portrait of Madame de Pompadour. Until 1965, about two- to three hundred golden lion tamarins were exported from Brazil each year. As the result of these pressures, the numbers of the golden lion tamarins, never really large, started a steady decline.

So much for their history—a tale that could, in its account of habitat destruction and uncontrolled capture of animals for pets, zoos, and laboratories, be retold for any number of other species. By 1966, those who cared about the fate of these beautiful little animals realized that a crisis existed. According to the best estimate, the remaining wild population had been reduced to about four hundred animals, though this was a rough figure at best; it is hard to count something that is about the size of a squirrel and leaps through the trees in somewhat the same manner. In even graver straits were the two subspecies of lion tamarins, the golden-headed and the golden-rumped, lovely black animals with golden patches in the corresponding spots. These were thought to be almost extinct.

When the American Association of Zoological Parks and Aquariums (AAZPA), the professional organization that guides and coordinates the efforts of North American zoos, held its annual meeting in 1966, the New York Zoological Society urged the Association to take action to save the lion tamarin. The result was an appeal to the Survival Services Commission of the International Union for the Conservation of Nature and Natural Resources (IUCN) to list the lion tamarin in the Red Data Book. Once a species is officially listed as endangered, it comes under a number of regulations, national and international, which make it easier to control its destiny. The following year the AAZPA and the International Union of the Directors of Zoological Gardens (IUDZG) pledged that their members would not import any lion tamarins from the wild, and the AAZPA sent a formal request to the Brazilian government for a ban on their exportation. This request was honored in 1968.

Two Brazilian biologists, Dr. Adelmar F. Coimbra-Filho and Dr. Alceo Magnanini, had meanwhile started a campaign to have their government set aside a substantial parcel of the remaining coastal forest as a reserve for golden lion tamarins, as well as the many other creatures that shared their habitat. They were to pursue this campaign for the next ten years.

No one expected the new reserve to appear overnight, however, and in the face of continuing habitat destruction it became clear that the real hope for the species lay in building a strong captive population. There were a fair number of animals scattered here and there amongst American zoos, but these animals, especially those born in captivity, had never bred very well. There were records of births as early as 1911 in Rotterdam, and in 1933 at the Bronx Zoo, but occasional births do not make a program.

Programs are made by a steady production of healthy babies, most of whom survive and breed, but both the birth and survival rates of golden lion tamarins were poor.

In 1972, John Perry, then Assistant Director of the National Zoo, and Donald Bridgewater of the Minnesota Zoo called a conference at the National Zoo, cosponsored by the Wild Animal Propagation Trust (since disbanded), the National Zoo, and the New York Zoological Society. At this conference, experts from Brazil and the United States pooled their knowledge of this handful of little furry creatures in the hope of assuring their continued existence.

From this meeting came a set of guidelines for the tamarin's care and housing. Changes were made in their diet. Wild tamarins, it was found, fancy an occasional bird's egg or lizard as well as insects and fruit. Because they need protein, their captive diet must include such snacks as baby mice or crickets in addition to their other foods. They are creatures of the sunlight, and if they are not to suffer from deficiency diseases need either direct sunshine (which also deepens the gold of their coats) or Vitamin D_3 supplements. Tamarins are susceptible to a wide range of viral infections, which they can contract both from other monkeys and from humans. So sensitive are they that exposure to a child recently inoculated against measles might result in an infection that could spread like wildfire and decimate a whole tarmarin colony. Today, these animals are shielded from the public and its assorted ills by glass and usually housed apart from other South American monkeys.

What the conference also revealed was that there was still a great deal unknown about the tamarin's reproductive behavior; were this mystery to go unsolved much longer, there could be little hope of producing those healthy tamarin babies. Hints from various sources indicated that some connection existed between the age at which young animals had been taken from their parents and their future success *as* parents or even their ability to become parents at all, but there was no definite information about this. On the encouraging side, experts felt that this difficulty was more likely to be a matter of their incomplete understanding of the little creatures' ecological and behavioral needs than a reaction to captivity, so that if the missing factor could be discovered, there should be no bar to successful breeding.

At this conference, a committee was formed that would watch over the efforts at tamarin breeding, set out recommendations for the care of the animals, and formulate a plan for research. The conference members also recommended support for Drs. Coimbra-Filho and Magnanini and their plans for the new Tijuca Bank of Lion Tamarins near Rio, where the two Brazilians were working to start a breeding facility stocked with animals they hoped to rescue from isolated pocket of forest slated for clearing, snatching them up ahead of the chain saw and bulldozer.

Under the direction of Dr. Devra Kleiman, at that time the reproduction zoologist, the National Zoo became the center for research on tamarin social life. Two tamarin families continued to live in the zoo as exhibit groups, but a larger colony, made up of animals from other zoos, came to live in a new building built especially for their use. Using both the exhibit and off-exhibit families, observers spent hour after hour watching quietly, keeping themselves as much a part of the background as possible so that the little monkeys would go on with their daily lives undisturbed. This was not always easy. As the tamarins became used to their human companions these did indeed become a part of the scenery, and the animals began to treat them as such, scampering onto an observer's shoulder to investigate his ear or to snatch pens and pencils, carrying them off to the highest point of the cage. Though such actions make it a little hard to remain cool and impersonal, details of tamarin social life slowly did begin to emerge.

What emerged from the notes of the observers was an interesting picture. While lion tamarins may seem to be only lovely balls of golden fur, inconsequential in the greater scheme of things, they are the possessors of a complex social system. They are monogamous; forming strong, life-long pair bonds. If set up in pairs at their manager's discretion, they may settle down nicely, but may sometimes also reject these partners. No one is sure how they select their mates in the wild—those activities are still hidden in the tree-tops—but a captive female placed with two males will only mate with one of them. She may play with a familiar male as if he were a brother, but she only responds to the courtship and mating overtures of one that is unfamiliar.

Once a pair has bonded they seem to decide that three is a crowd, and they must be established in their own territory, a space to call their own that is out of sight of other tamarin pairs. If they can catch a glimpse of the pair next door, they may sit and shriek defiance, producing an incredible volume of sound for such small animals. The presence of close neighbors, or at least visible ones, is a source of stress that may interfere with their getting on with their other affairs, such as reproduction.

Their shrieks are a source of stress to their keepers as well. At one time part of the National Zoo's colony had little windows in their cages that opened into the kitchen area, so that keepers and observers could keep an eye on what was happening inside. (Cage in this case, refers to an area like a small room with an adjoining porch for warm weather, nicely fitted with branches and with a dirt floor that can cushion falls or offer interesting scents, and nest boxes.) The animals soon found that by craning their necks, they could catch a glimpse of their neighbors and spent so much time calling insults across the kitchen that the windows had to be taped over. Later, when one-way glass was installed, a few animals would even watch the mirrored side of the windows, seeming to see a rival in their own reflections. One female spent so much

Fluffy golden lion tamarin juveniles play wonderful rollicking games among the branches.

time before the mirror, posing and gazing at her reflection, that she was nicknamed "Scarlett O'Hara."

For the wild creature, this antagonism helps to define a territory that serves to space out the good things of tamarin life, such as food and nest trees; it is also one reason why a wild population needs space.

If the young pair are healthy and content, they become parents, usually of twins but sometimes of triplets or singles. The tiny babies cling to their mother's fur for dear life; in fact they may have taken a good trip on her fur before they have completely emerged from the birth canal. Their early days are mostly spent nestled on their mother's back, almost invisible in her thick coat except when they move around to her front to nurse.

An occasional mother is very possessive of her babies, but after ten days or two weeks, most mothers find the growing infants a heavy load, to say nothing of the problem of the scratching of their sharp little claws. On the mother's instigation, the father, until now an interested onlooker and occasional groomer, becomes a helper. By sidling up to her mate and rubbing her back against a branch, the mother signals that it is high time he took a hand with the kids. The male presses his chest against the babies, allowing them to climb on board, and afterward carries them most of the time, except when they are feeding.

Baby tamarins grow fast and by the time they are four or five weeks old begin to leave their parents to explore and to test the new foods that their parents are eating, gradually beginning to find food for themselves. But if danger threatens, back they fly to safety, leaping aboard their parents and clutching tightly, lashing their tails, giving raspy calls, and sometimes trying to bite if the parents try to brush them off. Still, by thirteen weeks or so, they are weaned and quite independent.

It used to be more or less standard practice to take young tamarins away from their parents when they reached the stage of independence when many other kinds of young mammals do break that tie. But this, it developed, was the greatest mistake in their management, for the youngsters need to stay with their parents and learn from them how to care for babies. Toleration of a clinging, scratching, noisy infant does not come naturally. This means that they must remain part of the family until after another litter is born.

When, six months to a year after their own brith, a new litter appears on the scene, the juvenile tamarins become helpers, carrying babies, sharing food with them, and as they grow older playing wonderful rollicking games, dashing through the branches, pulling their long-suffering elders' tails, snatching food from under their noses. Young tamarins who have this experience are usually good parents in their turn; those without it may neglect or even turn on their infants.

One female appears in the records as the "Killer Female," known, with a complete lack of affection, as "Killer" for short. Killer had injured her first litter, but everyone hoped that she had mellowed when she gave birth to a second. However, only a day or so after their birth, she suddenly attacked one of her new offspring and threw the other to the ground. Her mate, like a good protective father, raced down to the screaming baby and tried to take it up, but this male had never had contact with an infant before. He sensed that he should pick it up, innate behavior taking him that far, but he had never learned the technique of pressing his chest to the baby so that it could grasp his fur. Instead, he kept his arms between himself and the infant, pressing it down so that it could not get a grip. Before the shocked observers could do anything to prevent it, Killer had dashed to the floor and dispatched the second baby. Needless to say, all of Killer's subsequent offspring were hand reared.

Such behavior, fortunately, is unsusual; life in a tamarin family is usually amicable until the day comes when the adults seem to feel that the juveniles should depart. Often it is the adult female who turns on her nearly adult daughter and sends her flying, sometimes even injuring her if she can not get far enough away. (Occasionally a daughter turns on her mother.) It is time now for the young animals, their education completed, so to speak, to set up on their own. They may be paired with another young animal, or possibly sent to another zoo.

Armed with this information about the tamarin's sex and social lives, breeders took a fresh look at their management; when this was combined with proper housing, diet, and medical care, there seemed no reason why the golden lion tamarin population should not take off and grow. Since they usually bear twin babies, sometimes twice a year, the potential was there for a rapid increase in the population. But in 1975, at a second tamarin conference, Dr. Kleiman reported that the future of the little animals still hung in the balance. In spite of better management, many of the original wild animals had died, infants still did not survive as well as they should, and in three years there had been a net increase of only five animals, while the wild population, in spite of its protected status, was even smaller than in 1972. Far from optimistic, Dr. Kleiman wrote at this time, "It is sad but typical, that we are only beginning to understand the complex social life of one of the most exquisite primates just as it disappears."

Still, there were a few hopeful signs. There were a number of young animals that were not yet of breeding age. The sex ratio that had stood at two males for every female had begun to even out. Animals had been gathered into a few colonies instead of being scattered through many zoos. The Tijuca Bank in Brazil now held forty-eight animals of all three subspecies and the promised reserve was nearing reality, finally finding its way through government red tape.

Although the outlook for the tamarins was far from hopeful in 1975, no one gave up, and persistence and the application of good management began to pay off. The captive tamarin population began to turn the corner. In 1975, there were seventy-two animals in North American zoos; by 1978 there were 120; in 1981 there were 261 and in 1983 almost four hundred in zoos around the world. The Tijuca Bank had its fiftieth birth; the Los Angeles Zoo its hundredth and the National Zoo its two-hundredth. Where there were only eight colonies in 1975, there are now more than thirty located all over the world, for as the population grew, pairs went out to set up new groups and to serve as insurance against disease wiping out any single colony.

Another important development in tamarin management was the establishment of a studbook for the golden lion tamarin. In 1972, Marvin Jones of the San Diego Zoo had assembled the data on the ancestry and location of all captive tamarins, making it possible to manage the animals as one population and to monitor the contribution of different genetic lines. *The International Studbook for the Golden Lion Tamarin* is now a substantial document, one of forty or so that exist for the better management of wild animals. Few people realize that such books exist, and if they are aware of studbooks at all, it is in relation to dogs, horses, or other domestic animals. But a studbook is much more than a source for the pedigree of a puppy, a paper that is usually filed away after the new owner notes how many champions are listed upon it. A good studbook is a working document that, in the hands of an expert, is of great importance to the future of the breed—or of the species. It is also an important source of information for planning matings. In the case of dogs a studbook is a guide to field-trial winners, breed-ring champions, or simply good, healthy puppies with the disposition and physique that have made that breed famous. It is an aid to the prospective breeder in avoiding hip dysplasia, juvenile cataract, ingrown eyelids, or whatever other genetic weaknesses the breed may harbor.

The same is now true for the studbooks for wild animals. Once primarily a source of pedigrees that guaranteed that what the buyer had was, for example, a pure-bred Siberian tiger, they are becoming guidelines to the health and genetic diversity of the species. Each of the studbooks for exotic animals has the backing of a major zoo here or abroad, and their keepers are increasingly called on for advice in selecting specimens, arranging matings, and on the idiosyncrasies of the behavior of various species, each of which has its own quirks when it comes to family life.

The International Studbook for the Golden Lion Tamarin is now maintained at the National Zoo by Dr. Kleiman. The first sections give immediate information on all the animals living when the current edition was compiled, listing their parentage, location, breeding record, their experience as baby sitters, the presence or absence of a genetically determined hernia, which affects some animals. Stillbirths and abortions appear, for these are pertinent information in management. There is a record of deaths and transfers of animals that have taken place since the last edition. A larger section lists all of the golden lion tamarins, including those now living, that have passed through the world's zoos since 1960, making it possible to trace any animal's ancestry back to the first wild caught individuals.

To take a sample entry:

Number	Sex	Studbook Name House Name House Number	Date of Birth or Arrival	Site	Own	Male Parent	Female Parent	Death Date	Comments
78–20b	M	Washington 113/102381 /8062–45 "Pele" /420	2.6.78 26.7.79 28.2.80	Washington Oklahoma City Wichita	WA OK OK	75–7a	76–16b		1(2) + Visited Dallas

This translates quite easily. 78-20b means that animals was the 20th birth in 1978, and was the second of twins (the first born twin was 20a). It is male (M), and its studbook name is Washington 113. Its number at the National Zoo was 102381, which was changed when it was transferred to Oklahoma City in 1979, and again when it went to Wichita in 1980. It was owned by the National Zoo orginially (WA), but was given to the Oklahoma City Zoo which still owns it, but loaned it to Wichita. Its father was 75-7a and its mother was 76-16b. "I(2)" means that it had at least a month's experience in the care of a younger litter of two infants, and + means that it was examined for hereditary diaphramatic hernia and found clear.

"Visited Dallas" is another part of the story. On his way from the Oklahoma City Zoo to Wichita's Sedgwick County Zoo, 78-20b passed through Dallas's airport and, while between planes somehow or other managed to get himself loose. A tamarin on the loose is about as easy to catch as a greased pig, or perhaps more fittingly, a will-o'-the-wisp, and the helpful souls who tried to catch him never dreamed that something as small, fluffy, and innocent appearing could move like smoke and bite like a fiend. By the time that 78-20b was finally cornered, returned to his crate, and sent on his way, there were a number of bloody fingers in Dallas, and the episode appears in the Studbook as a cryptic comment, "Visited Dallas."

In 1981, the owners and holders of golden lion tamarins signed an agreement, setting up an elected committee that would guide the future destiny of the little monkeys, a group that might well be considered as trustees or guardians, for it is their duty to see that their charges are properly cared for, that new captive colonies are set up in the best locations with the proper animals, and that we can continue to learn from them.

In 1983, the tamarin story came full circle. On November 6, Dr. Kleiman, who is now the National Zoo's Assistant Director for Research and Education, boarded a plane at Washington's National Airport bound for Rio de Janeiro. Watching Dr. Kleiman that morning, it seemed that she really didn't need a plane, that she might easily have flown to Rio on the wings of her own exuberance, because, carefully crated and traveling on the plane with her, were fifteen very special golden lion tamarins. The long-promised reserve—the Poço das Antas Biological Preserve—had become a reality and the time had come when some captive-born animals could be returned to Brazil for release into their native forests. The goal of at least one captive propagation program was about to be realized.

But the tamarins were not to have immediate freedom. At the Rio de Janeiro Primate Center a team of scientists, including Dr. Benjamin Beck, a primatologist from the National Zoo and Dr. Coimbra-Filho, for whom this event must have been the realization of a dream, were waiting to start the re-education of these little creatures. This phase of the program was as much a cooperative and international effort as the rest of the tamarin program had been. Most important, it had the full backing of the Brazilian government. The funds that supported this phase of the venture came from many sources, including the Smithsonian Institution, the National Geographic Society, the World Wildlife Fund, the Wildlife Preservation Trust, and the Friends of the National Zoo. All of the zoos that hold or breed golden lion tamarins were contributors to the project in one way or another, and the pioneering animals came from a number of zoos, including the National, Brookfield, Los Angeles, and Kings Island Zoo in Ohio.

With the assistance of young biologists from Brazil and the United States, Dr. Beck began to expand a teaching process he had begun before the animals left the United States. Wild tamarins search for insects, small vertebrates, and fruit under bark and in

At the National Zoological Park, Brazil-bound golden lion tamarins practice searching for their food under the watchful eyes of Dr. Devra Kleiman and Dr. Benjamin Beck.

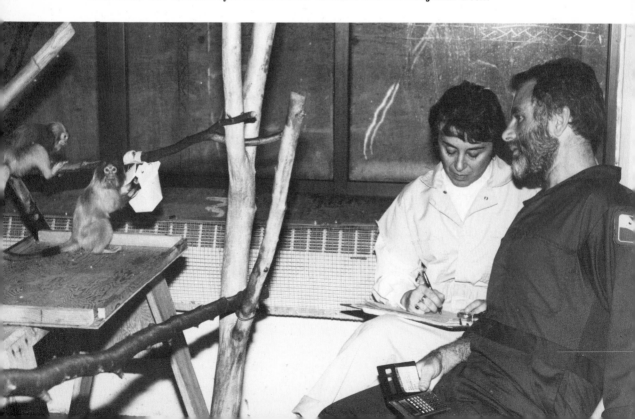

Dr. Kleiman (left) loads golden lion tamarins and their equipment for the trip to the airport. National Zoo staff members, Gene Maliniak and Mike Deal, and Dr. Beck assist.

curled-up leaves, hidden in crevices or air plants, or high in the trees under hanging foliage. These captive-born animals, two or three generations removed from the wild, were accustomed to chopped fruit and chilled and lethargic crickets; they did not even recognize an unpeeled banana as food! Slowly, patiently, hiding food in unlikely palces and in unfamiliar containers, introducing live food that hopped or flew and native fruits that must be opened, the scientists encouraged the animals to hunt for their meals. Branches placed in their cages gave them plenty of opportunity to climb and leap, helping them to sharpen their agility and gain greater strength.

Finally, the animals chosen for release were moved to a huge temporary enclosure at the point in the forest where the doors would at last be opened. This enclosure took in a chunk of the native forest complete with natural foods, so that it was a sample of the environment that the animals would soon occupy. Here they lived for another month, for their final acclimation.

In May of 1984, the cage door was opened. The films of the great moment are very moving. A hatch in the top of the cage rises and, after a moment, a little golden head emerges to eye level and a pair of bright eyes surveys the world outside. The head returns to the cage, but a slender paw remains on the edge. A moment later, another head appears, then ducks back, and one can almost imagine a whispered conference. Suddenly, a tamarin climbs out and looks about at a world that holds no wire or glass or any hindrance between it and the tall trees. To the delight of the watching biologists, the rest of its family slowly follows and in a few minutes, the whole group is vanishing into the forest, followed by the cheers of their audience.

Not all the tamarins that have been released have survived, but most have, and although the losses are mourned, the success of the others has been cause for great satisfaction. The released young animals, especially, are now impossible to distinguish from wild ones.

But does this mean that golden lion tamarins are now safe? Only time will tell. Although the Poço das Antas Reserve protects a part of the remaining wild population, and provides a place to release the captive animals, it is smaller than was originally projected. Of even that smaller area, many acres were deforested before the reserve could be established. In addition, adjoining forests which still harbor some of the remaining wild tamarin population are fast being cleared.

Dr. James Dietz, a research fellow at the National Zoo, is working at the reserve with Brazilian scientists, conducting field studies that will help with the management of the tamarin population, and training young Brazilians in field techniques. They study local plants and the ways in which the tamarins make use of their habitat. Based on such studies, the field workers plant native trees in the deforested sections in an attempt to provide the proper habitat for more tamarins. The Brazilians also try to capture animals from areas outside the reserve, where the forest is being cleared, in order to move them to safety.

Meanwhile, Dr. Dietz's wife, Lou Anne, who is an educational specialist, has been conducting a program among the reserve's human neighbors, teaching them about these wonderful little animals that are to be found only in their home state. Speaking at schools and churches, and using posters, films, radio, television, she is reaching out to the entire community. The thrust of the program is not only to protect the tamarins, but their habitat as well. DON'T DESTROY OUR HOMES says the poster, another way of emphasizing the value of the tropical forest. (Interestingly, the local people feel that destruction of the forests is one of their most serious problems.) Ultimately, hers may be the most important effort of all.

For some time to come, the captive population will remain the golden lion tamarin's real safeguard, a back-up for a species that is found in only one small spot on the globe. We have yet to be sure that reintroduction is possible over a longer period of time and that this reserve can furnish protection for enough animals. With about four hundred animals, the captive population is considered of sound size for a long-term program. Now is the time for refinement of the methods, a time when the principles guiding the long-term management of a captive population will be tested.

Ten years ago, the idea that the day would come when there would be enough golden lion tamarins in zoos to consider their release in Brazil was regarded as the wildest kind of pie-in-the-sky vision. It seemed impossible that there would even be enough animals to maintain the captive population. The thriving population now in zoos has been made possible by a relatively new kind of zoo breeding program, which considers all members of a captive species as a whole, studies their needs, and applies what has been learned persistently, methodically, and patiently to their management. And this works, given a little bit of luck and a whole lot of faith.

PLANS FOR SURVIVAL

In the winter of 1983, the National Zoo's female giant panda, Ling-Ling, became acutely ill. For several days her life was in danger, and on television, on the radio, and in newspapers all over the country, appeared the guarded news bulletins from the Zoo. An anxious public awaited the news of the fate of *their* panda. Ling-Ling, always something of a celebrity, displaced affairs of state and even the local political figures in the news.

An avalanche of mail poured in, bag after bag of it, piling into drifts in the mail room and behind the information desk. There were cards and notes from individual children. Children called, asking that someone pat Ling-Ling for them. Whole school classes sent drawings of pandas bearing their hopes for her recovery. Adults expressed concern and sometimes offered advice, relating things that had cured their own infections, from using certain antibiotics to eating kiwi fruit. Fortunately, the crisis passed; thanks to prompt diagnosis and very skillful treatment of her kidney infection by the Zoo's veterinary staff, Ling-Ling began what was to be a complete recovery. Before long, she was cruching bamboo and regaining her lost weight, very much her old self again.

At about the same time, a small item appeared in newspapers and magazines across the country describing the critical situation facing the remaining wild pandas in China. Because of a massive die-off of bamboo in their habitat, many of the thousand or so wild pandas were in danger of starvation. Bamboo, which is the panda's staple food, blossoms only once in its extended lifetime. After it blossoms, it sets seed and the parent plant dies. Since most of the plants in any area blossom and die at the same time, there is a dearth of bamboo until the new plants get a start. At one time when such a die-off occurred the giant pandas could simply move to another area, searching for another kind of bamboo. But today they are restricted to small areas with limited resources, and such moves are impossible.

Concern over the welfare of the species was well founded. In the mid-seventies, during such a die-off, 138 pandas did starve, a loss of about ten per cent of an already reduced population. During the 1983 crisis, both the World Wildlife Fund International

A black panther is not a distinct species, but simply a leopard in a beautiful black coat. There may be black and spotted cubs in the same litter.

and the New York Zoological Society, organizations that help support panda research in China, publicized the plight of the pandas, appealing for funds to cover the cost of flying food into the mountains, but until World Wildlife took advantage of President Reagan's visit to China in 1984, and inspired Mrs. Reagan to launch a "Pennies for Pandas" campaign, the response was limited to those on the organizations' mailing lists. News items in the media brought no such expression of public concern as that evoked by Ling-Ling's illness.

In part, this is a reflection of the old story that a crisis on the other side of the world seems remote, while the event next door arouses our emotions. (And what, in any case, can one *do* about an event a world away?) But it also reflects the difference between our perception of an individual and of a species. Individual animals have reality—a panda named Ling-Ling, a tiger named Mohini, a gorilla named Tomoka—whereas a species is an abstraction called *Ailuropoda melanoleuca*, or *Panthera tigris*, or *Gorilla gorilla*, unpronounceable names that are something for the scientists to worry about. For most of us, it is much easier to love and care for something we can see and visit and photograph than for an abstraction beyond our ken.

But species are what it is all about. It is the diversity of species that makes the world such a fascinating place. Think of the dozens of different kinds of fish on a coral reef, the dozens of different flowers in a meadow, the different bird voices on a spring morning. Our concern there is not for this daisy or that parrot fish or a particular warbler; it is that members of their whole wonderful group continue to exist.

If, for a moment, we revisit our biology classrooms, we may remember that a species is more than just a group of animals that look alike. Irish setters all look alike, but they are not a species. Male and female Eclectus parrots were long considered to be two species because they look so very different; the males are a brilliant green while their females are soft maroon. When these birds were finally found sharing nests together and rearing young together, it was clear that they belonged together, members of one species. Visitors to the National Zoo in the fall of 1984 often stand and scan the eagle cage looking for the bird. In fact, he is often sitting before their eyes, but because he is still a juvenile, he is just a big, brown bird, lacking the gleaming white head and tail that will be his upon maturity.

The simplest criteria of a species is that its members will choose as mates *only* other members of the same species, and will have offspring like themselves. Irish setters will joyfully mate with anything from a boxer to a corgi and produce pups that look like anything in between, or like what they are, dogs—*Canis familiaris*. A bald eagle seeking a mate has no interest, except perhaps an antagonistic one, in a golden eagle. A giant panda has ears only for the bleating of a female panda. And the little grey cygnet is no Ugly Duckling, but a true regal white swan in the making.

In their search for a proper mate, animals are directed by cues of color or sound, scent or behavior that tell them that they are selecting one of their own kind, and not wasting precious time and energy on a union that is destined to fail. Mallards, teal, pintails, and others of the dabbling ducks often form mixed flocks in winter. Late winter is the time for courtship, and the drakes are at their sleek and colorful best, the males of each species very distinct in their feather pattern, while the females are, as always, brown and mottled, looking very much alike to even an experienced bird watcher.

But watch—a mallard preens behind his wing with a sharp stylized gesture that is quite unlike his routine feather care, drawing the duck's attention to the iridescent blue wing patch, the speculum. She may be interested and circle round to face him, or swim on past nodding her lowered head, indicating her acceptance, or she may paddle busily on her way as if he did not exist. A pintail jerks head and tail toward each other as if he were trying to bend himself double, and half opens his wings, uttering a shrill whistle. A female falls in to swim close and may cement the bond by making a great fuss, inciting him to drive off other drakes. A teal faces a duck as if he were drinking, tossing up a shower of drops to sparkle from his bill.

Everywhere is commotion. The drakes are cruising about, sometimes several in line, displaying to more or less interested ducks going through routines that may use some of the same movements, though never in the same sequence. Females may or may not respond right away, but by the time migration begins in the spring almost every female mallard will fly north followed by a male mallard, each pintail in the company of another pintail, as they have for centuries.

It is true that many drakes, especially mallards, will mate with anything that quacks. It is the female that makes the choice, responding only to the drake that makes the "right" movements in the "right" sequence and that has the "right" plumage for her species. Even experts makes mistakes, and hybrid ducks do turn up both in the zoo and the in the wild, but these youngsters rarely breed themselves. They are likely to have inherited a mixed set of markings or signals, or they may have a different time table for breeding than one of the parent species, or have inherited the wrong call for their young, or simply lay infertile eggs. These failures assure that the hybrid line ends with that duck and protects the integrity of the species.

All of this happens because each member of a species has the same number of chromosomes and a similar arrangement of genes. These provide the information that is passed from generation to generation, assuring that each new creature will look and behave much like its parents. This gene combination is the end product of a long evolutionary history that has fitted that particular species to deal effectively with certain environmental conditions and to fill a certain place in its habitat. Giant pandas are equipped to feed on bamboo and to live in the cold, damp mountains where the bamboo forests grow. They are specialists, limited by their very expertise in a certain habitat to

relying on that habitat only, their fate tied to their surroundings. Other species are generalists, as are mallards and raccoons, able to adapt to and take advantage of a changing environment. Whatever each species' solution may be, its particular combination of genes, or its gene pool, is protected by the fact that its members do not normally mate with members of other species.

One rhino or elephant or panda, no matter how beautiful and valuable, is only a sample of its species and can be replaced as long as the species exists, but once the species itself is gone its gene pool can never be reconstituted. Genetic engineers today are accomplishing marvels, but even if they should one day be able to create species to order, it is unlikely that they could or would be able to replace more than a very few of the species that are now endangered, if only because the expense would be prohibitive. Captive propagation is concerned with the preservation of gene pools, although this preservation is tied to the welfare of individual animals.

Captive breeding programs can be divided into two kinds—breeding for exhibit animals and breeding for species preservation, although it is impossible to make a hard and fast distinction between the two. A great many important exhibit animals are also endangered, and most of the requirements for breeding success are common to both. Exhibit animals in this sense come from species that are not endangered, although there are a number of professionals who feel that all tropical species will soon be endangered, regardless of their present status, and might as well be considered so today. Many of these animals could be replaced from the wild, but because of costs and various restrictions, must be replaced by zoo-bred animals. Breeding for exhibit means keeping an armadillo in the armadillo enclosure and a common zebra in the zebra paddock, or finding a good substitute. These programs are often relatively short term in their outlook,

Captive propagation aimed at preserving species operates in a much longer time frame, fifty to one hundred and fifty years, or even longer, and so it involves a far greater degree of commitment of time, space, and resources than breeding for exhibit replacement. More of these animals cannot be taken from the wild except to save them from certain destruction or to meet very specific needs for breeding their species. As we shall see, such programs call for far greater numbers of animals to assure healthy future generations, and all of these factors make substantial differences in their planning.

The first step in any form of captive propagation involves selecting species to be part of the programs and setting priorities among them. This may sound rather obvious, but, when decisions have to be made about endangered species, this can be one of the most difficult questions that has to be answered. In an earlier day, say before 1950, the problem was easier, for there were fewer species in danger.

Although a mallard drake may mate with females of other species, the resulting hybrid youngsters rarely mate successfully.

Efforts at preserving species through captive propagation are not new. There have been a number of successful ones, the outcome of the concern and dedication of certain individuals and institutions. Thus, we will always credit the Duke of Bedford with recognizing the plight of Père David's deer back in 1900, and acting to save it; the Polish naturalist Jan Sztolcman and zoologist Jan Zabinski, with preserving the European bison through two World Wars and their attendant revolutions; Hawaiian farmer, Harold Shipman, and later Sir Peter Scott, the noted ornithologist who founded the Wildfowl Trust at Slimbridge, England, with taking action to save the Nene goose around 1950. The world owes such individuals a debt of gratitude. But today there are so many endangered species that the interest of individuals is not enough.

Although estimates vary and lists differ, there are certainly no fewer than 437 species of birds and 287 of mammals that are rare, threatened, or endangered, and the list is growing rapidly. Not all of these are good candidates for captive propagation; some can only be protected within their own habitats. Others can benefit from the back-up of a captive population, while still other species will only survive in captivity. Even among these, there have to be choices. Because long-term programs call for substantial numbers of animals, North American zoos, with the best will in the world, cannot house more than one hundred to two hundred of such species in their present facilities.

Recognizing this, the AAZPA is attempting to address captive propagation through a program of Species Survival Plans (SSP) that was introduced at their annual meeting in 1981. This plan grew out of the recommendations of several international inter-zoo conferences on captive breeding beginning in 1972, as well as the encouragement of the Survival Service of the International Union for the Conservation of Nature (IUCN) and a substantial part of the scientific community. Since then, the plans have gone steadily forward, and by 1984, some thirty-three species have been chosen for inclusion.

Its Wildlife Conservation and Management Committee makes the selections for the AAZPA, receiving suggestions from AAZPA members and initiating some themselves. In their deliberations, this committee has had to answer some knotty questions, both philosophical and practical. Has a rhino really greater value to the world than a mouse? Can we justify using space for one species of large animal when this same space would support several kinds of a smaller beast? What about the relative claims of mammals, birds, or reptiles? How do you choose between two species of monkeys or two of antelopes?

In an attempt to answer these questions and place the new plans on a practical basis, they have developed criteria for their choices. The species must be threatened in its

Ruffed lemurs are endangered in their native Madagascar, but have a growing captive population, exemplified by these gnomelike quadruplets.

native habitat, if not actually endangered. There must be professionals available who can manage the program. There must be enough of the species already in captivity to start the program. It is true that these criteria tip the scales in the early selections toward large mammals and birds. Because of their size, these need space and may be the first to feel the impact of habitat changes, and they are highly visible and often hunted. Because of their value as exhibit animals, there are often many already in captivity.

But even if there are none of its members in captivity at present, a species may be considered if it is in imminent danger of extinction, or it is rare and the only representative of a taxonomic family or genus. Of all these criteria, endangered status is the first concern.

But even with these guidelines, selection is still difficult. The plight of the world's rhinos serves as an example. There are five species of rhinos and all are endangered to a greater or lesser degree in their habitats in Africa and Asia. Their status is due partly to the drastic changes that have taken place in their habitats, and partly to a brisk demand for rhino horn and other parts to use as aphrodisiacs and various folk medicines. The demand for these is greatest in Asia, but with increasing populations of Asian origin in the United States, rhino horn is now being smuggled into our country.

An Indian rhino's deeply folded skin resembles armor plate. This one has worn its horn down by rubbing it on trees and other objects.

The horns of these amiable white rhinos would be worth thousands of dollars on the black market in the Persian Gulf.

In addition, the flow of oil money into Yemen and other Arab nations has created a demand for such highly prized status symbols as daggers with rhino horn hilts. Yemen, to its credit, has bowed to pressure from several world conservation organizations and banned the import of the rhino horn, but smuggling is an established way of life in the Persian Gulf and Indian Ocean. The price of rhino horn has at times reached $16,000 a kilo, and in a region where annual incomes run around $200, economics tell their own tale.

A rhino is not just a rhino; there are five species that are placed in four genera and are quite different in appearance. The Indian rhino sports only one horn and its thick hide is so creased and folded that it seems to be dressed in armor plate complete with rivets. India and Nepal have made valiant efforts to protect their wildlife, and Indian rhinos now have a relatively stable population of around two thousand. However, this is probably about as large as this population can grow. Most, if not all, of the animals are now living within parks; they are long lived, territorial beasts, and there is room in the parks for only so many. There is no way that these parks can be made any larger. There are seventy-one of these rhinos in the world's zoos, with twenty-two living in North America.

The Javan rhino is similar (it belongs to the same genus as the Indian); it is a little smaller, with a smaller horn on the males, while females are usually hornless. It was once found over a large part of southeast Asia but is now to be found only in Java, where probably fewer than sixty remain. Indonesia has one of the densest human populations in the world, and the few remaining rhinos are squeezed into the reed beds and tall grass of a small park.

The Sumatran rhino has two horns, is half the size of the Indian rhino, and has a good deal of bristly hair on its body. The few remaining animals, scattered in patches of hill forest across southeast Asia and into Borneo, are all that remain of the species of the great beast depicted on the cave walls at Lascaux; they once had a much wider distribution. There are fewer than two hundred Sumatran rhinos left in the world, and few of either the Javan or Sumatran rhinos are to be found in zoos.

Africa boasts two species of rhinos, the black and the white. Both have two horns, but in spite of their names the black is not particularly black nor is the white particularly white. White rhinos are rather mild-mannered grazers, with a broad square lip that caused the Dutch settlers to name it the "wijd" or wide-lipped rhino. Tipping the scales at up to three tons, they are the largest land mammal after the elephant. With a population in South Africa of around 2,800 and growing, the southern subspecies of the white rhino has the strongest position in the wild of any of the rhinos, and are present in zoos in substantial numbers. (The northern subspecies is extremely rare, both in the wild and in zoos, but only recently has the government of Zaire, where most of the animals are located, shown interest in captive breeding.) In 1981, there were 172 white rhinos in North America zoos and 539 worldwide, partly because zoos have been taking in animals from Africa that have had to be removed from parks to prevent overcrowding, and would probably otherwise have been shot.

Black rhinos are browsers and have a pointed, somewhat prehensile upper lip useful for tearing leaves from twigs. This is the animal with the reputation for agressiveness and general bad temper, a reputation that may be deserved, but which probably results from the rather poor eyesight that makes it prudent for a rhino to charge rather than to wait and ask questions. They have suffered acutely from poaching. The population in Kenya in 1979 had fallen from an estimated 15,000 to 1,500, while the number of

Experience with zoo-born Andean condors have aided the current efforts to breed California condors in captivity.

black rhinos in the great Serengeti Park in Tanzania has fallen from about two thousand to only a hundred. Fifty-six live in North American zoos.

What should be done about rhinos? Thomas Foose, Conservation Coordinator for the AAZPA, presented the rationale for the rhino SSPs in a way that illustrates the problems and frustrations inherent in the process. There is space for about three hundred rhinos, give or take a few, in American zoos. Logic would suggest that this space should be filled by Indian, black, and Sumatran rhinos. All are shrinking species, and each belongs to a distinct and unique genus. The behavior and needs for care of at least the black and the Indian are familiar. In fact, these three were the final choices.

There is one complication to this picture. There are no Sumatran rhinos in North America, but there are a lot of white rhinos, the one species with a strong wild population. However, no one knows how long white rhinos will continue to thrive, and they are another distinct, unique life form. A possible solution appeared in the fact that white rhinos, unlike the other species, prefer to live in herds and breed better in that sort of arrangement. Rather than keeping them in a regular zoo situation, usually in pairs, perhaps some will be placed in a semi-wild herd on a ranch, somewhere in the western United States, that would not be unlike their homeland. That way, they could be preserved, and space opened up for the Sumatran rhino, if breeding stock could be obtained. Besides, here the white rhinos are and must be cared for.

Decisions about such species as rhinos, however, may be simple compared to those about the really rare and unique creature that needs protection, but must be taken from the wild in order to receive it. These decisions are often a source of controversy. Such animals may be rare to zoos because they have a history of being hard to keep. Species such as lemurs, the beautiful and fascinating Madagascan primates, and tarsiers, tiny, big-eyed, elfin members of the primate family from the Philippines and Malasia, are both rare and difficult, and give cause for concern. No one can justify bringing rare animals from the wild without some hope that this will benefit their species, but animal husbandry and medical care in zoos have made such tremendous advances in recent years that, in a case of a drastically dwindling population, many scientists and conservationists feel that a few of the remaining animals should be taken from the wild to start a captive program.

Debate raged over whether to protect the California condor through captive propagation as well as habitat protection, with scientists and conservationists appearing in both camps. Not until the species plunged to thirty individuals did the U.S. Fish and Wildlife Service, with the backing of the Audubon Society and the American Ornithologist's Union, come down on the side of captive propagation, a decision that is showing results in the form of hand-reared condors at the Los Angeles and San Diego zoos.

Once the species for a captive propagation program has been identified, the animals for the breeding colonies must be located and gathered together. Even before the advent of the SSPs, zoos had realized that they must begin to cooperate in breeding programs and had started to change from their traditional practice of selling animals to each other to a system of loans and trades. Loans allow an animal to travel to another zoo for a season, or for several seasons, breed as part of the group there, but still be owned by the original zoo. Either the creature returns home at some time, or one or more of its offspring come back to the parent institution. Sometimes, the loan becomes a trade— my oryx for your gazelle.

Such trades and loans have resulted in many zoo babies. A pair of orangutans at the National Zoo lived together for eleven years in a perfectly friendly but purely platonic relationship. In an attempt to improve matters, "Butch," the male, went traveling. He was first loaned to the Franklin Park Zoo in Boston, where he did no better as a sire, but when he was shipped off to the Cheyenne Mountain Zoo, in Colorado Springs, he found a female that must have pleased him, for he fathered half a dozen babies. Meanwhile, "Jennie," the mate that he had spurned, bore seven offspring to her new mate, "Archie," acquired by trading a gorilla to another institution.

Shipping animals from one place to another may sound like a risky procedure, but although it has its hazards, it is has become a rather routine matter. Many animals, even big ones, may travel by air, cutting down the time that they must be crated. Crating a rhino or other large animal involves placing the crate in its enclosure, sometimes months in advance of the shipping date, so that it becomes familiar. The animal is fed there, and as time passes, you may see the rhino stretched out in its crate, sleeping peacefully.

When shipping time approaches, the zoo's registrar, or whoever is responsible for such matters in the zoo, works out the best route for that animal. This does involve some odd considerations. Giraffes, with their long necks, may stand eighteen feet tall, and, combined with truck and crate, cannot clear some highway underpasses. Some airlines are reluctant to accept monkeys or venomous snakes as passengers. And unlike other baggage, these shipments have to be fed and watered and kept warm or cool during transit, so often another zoo along the route is alerted to meet the plane and see that all is going well. Occasionally, a baby animal, or one that is of great value, has to be hand carried in the passenger compartment for safety, and this entails other arrangements, and sometimes some fast talking. But shipments are so common that they now move very smoothly.

This is just as well, because there will be even more animals on the move in the future. The SSPs will enlarge and continue these loans, which are already substantial. At any given time, the National Zoo might have as many as three hundred and fifty animals out on loans and house two hundred and twenty-five creatures from other zoos, the result of arrangements in effect at that time with ninety-eight other institutions. But

A young giraffe, en route to a new home, is urged into a traveling crate by National Zoo staff members.

the SSPs will change the form of some of these cooperative arrangements. While zoos have evolved a high degree of cooperation, and some have tried forming breeding consortia for better species management—the Bronx Zoo, the Philadelphia Zoo, and the National Zoo for example, often working closely together—the agreements have not usually been based on considerations of the total North American population of any species.

SSPs will be based on the total population. They will be coordinated, rather than cooperative, plans. They will operate under management agreements that bring together the resources of all the zoos that agree to join in, in an effort to protect these selected species. These follow a pattern similar to the agreements that were used so successfully in the golden lion tamarin program. A species coordinator and elected management committee will decide which animals shall be bred, when, where, and how often, and zoos that take part agree to manage their animals in accordance with the recommendations of this committee.

Successful management of this kind calls for accurate information on what animal is where, on how many there are in zoos, on how well they reproduce, and how old they are. Even before the advent of the SSPs, it became clear that increased emphasis on breeding and greater cooperation called for better information than was available through the zoological "old boy" network that had been the favored route for the exchange of information in the past. Curators needed to find homes for young animals and mates for older ones. They needed information on new species that they were considering for their collections—where these could be found, how successful others had been with them. It was very difficult for anyone to tell what the true status of any captive species was, for some zoo's records systems were relatively incomplete, and because of differences in practice, few were standardized.

At the AAZPA Annual Meeting, in 1973, Dr. Ulysses S. Seal and D.G. Makey proposed a central computerized file for all animals in all North American zoos, a number that runs around 30,000. This proposal was so obviously an idea whose time had come that the project was endorsed with enthusiasm, and the International Species Inventory System (ISIS) was launched. (International may have seemed a little visionary then, but it has since become an accurate term.) Mammals were to be included first, then birds, and later the reptiles. Farther in the future, there were plans to add amphibians and fish as well as some of the physiological data that interest zoo veterinarians, such as blood studies and hormone levels.

By 1982, one hundred and fifty zoos and primate centers, most of them in Canada and the United States, but including a growing number of foreign zoos, were reporting information on the members of the species they held—their origins, numbers, sexes, and breeding records—to ISIS at its home at the Minnesota Zoo. The system has been dubbed by the press, "the international dating bureau," which, in one way, is a fair enough name. If a curator has a lone rhino or a pair of incompatible chimpanzees, he can now turn to ISIS for help in finding mates. Because the computer can cross-refer and search its files, instead of locating a single mate for his lone rhino, a curator might find two or three that he could choose from. He would be able to select the one that was the best match in age, perhaps one that was a proven breeder, and one that was unlikely to turn out to be his rhino's first or second cousin. The day may come soon when this might even be a wild rhino from Africa. There is consideration of entering black rhinos from certain African parks (and tigers from Indian ones) into the ISIS files as a part of their proper management in the wild.

Another value of ISIS is that, as data accumulates, it can serve somewhat the same function as a studbook. There are only about forty species covered by studbooks at present, and anyone wishing to start one has to meet the standards of the AAZPA, the International Studbook Coordinator in London, the IUDZG, and the IUCN, as well as demonstrating institutional support. Because of this process, although SSPs call for official studbooks for each species in the plans, they will probably never be set up for all other species. There are plans to feed some of the studbook data into the ISIS files which, although they do not go as far back in time as a studbook, are sometimes more current.

ISIS is essential to the success of the SSPs because not only can it provide accurate information on numbers, locations, and relationships, but the operators of the ISIS computer can correlate this information and build models—such as a model of what will happen in twenty or fifty years if each lioness in the United States has five cubs, or four cubs, or one every three years. These models, as well as statistical analyses of births and deaths and other data, result in a much more accurate picture of the present and future situation of a given species than could ever be found from card files tucked away in individual zoos. ISIS's usefulness has grown steadily as data has accumulated and membership has increased, and its importance is tremendous. Without such a central file, coordination of breeding programs would be impossible; in fact it would be difficult to make the most basic assumptions about the current state of a given species.

To return to the time frame, SSPs are designed to meet two ends. One is the idea of rescue and return, exemplified by the golden lion tamarin and the California condor. This uses the captive population, or young animals taken for rearing in safety, to provide new recruits for a dwindling wild population. The period of captivity for some may be relatively short—the first California condors may be released as early as 1985—although a captive population must be maintained as insurance. Or it may be a long time until enough safe habitat can be guaranteed to warrant returning a species to its original homeland.

The other aim is to provide permanent sanctuary for species that no one really believes will find a place in the wild in the foreseeable future, but without which the world would be a much poorer place. Many big animals may fall into this category; probably tigers, possibly rhinos, conceivably even Asian elephants.

SSPs are still very new. As of 1983, only four were truly off and running, complete with studbooks, management groups, and master plans. These four are the groups for the golden lion tamarin, the Siberian tiger, the Przewalski's horse, and the Asian lion. Others are making rapid progress, and, probably inevitably, a few are trailing. They are also creating a great deal of reassessment and evaluation in the zoo world as they bring home the reality that, endangered or not, SSP or not, captive breeding requires certain measures for long-term success, and that this is a matter of concern for all zoos acting together.

One detects a note of "We're finally doing something about this!" New people are coming to the fore in the profession, and there is somewhat more emphasis on certain fields of scientific knowledge than in the past. There is a certain professional excitement, usually well concealed under professional language, but there none the less. Eventually, this is bound to surface in the zoo itself, and gradually affect the image of zoos, perhaps carrying some of the excitement to the public.

However, it is only fair to present possible problems SSPs will face. One is expense. William Conway's estimate of twenty-five billion dollars includes such items as feeding tigers, at about $2,000 a year each (about $1,200,000 for all the Siberian tigers now in captivity), salaries, support for ISIS, costs of transporting animals. This will be felt in even a large zoo's budget and zoos with municipal support may face quite a task convincing taxpayers of the value of programs that seem designed to help someone else and even take animals away from their zoos. Most zoos draw a substantial part of their income from gate receipts; in fact, they rely on these to a far greater extent that does any other kind of museum or park. They will have to face the problem of explaining to an irritable public that there are now six of the same kind of crane to be seen in the zoo but no gorilla because the gorilla's services were needed elsewhere.

Zoos that take part in a plan surrender control of their animals—although on a voluntary basis with the right to withdraw—to the management committee for that species. Wild animals, to be perfectly crass, are worth a lot of money; in the past, many a zoo has balanced its budget by the sale of young animals to other zoos. It may be difficult for smaller zoos that do not have the backing of support societies to give up this source of income. Eventually, these needs may have to be met through a higher level of government funding. By 1981, $662,000 in federal funds had been requested for the California condor project, in addition to funds from the two zoos involved and the conservation organizations backing the project. And that is only the start for a program that will eventually run into millions.

Another hindrance is found in regulations that cover the movement of animals about the nation and the world, which, while necessary for their protection and that of others, do complicate arrangements for breeding groups. The movements of wild animals are of interest to some twenty-seven agencies of the United States government which are charged with preventing diseases from entering the country and infecting domestic animals, or protecting animals' welfare, or enforcing regulations designed to protect endangered forms of life. Foreign governments feel an equal interest, but perhaps in different diseases or species. In overseas, or even domestic, shipments, observing these regulations takes time and generates quantities of paper.

Once, when a golden lion tamarin was sent from the Tulsa Zoo to Belfast, Northern Ireland, an inquisitive zoo employee eyed the tamarin and the package of documents, and placed the documents on the scale. They weighed well over a pound, as much as the animal they concerned. There was a letter of instructions for the tamarin's care and a letter that guaranteed payment to the airline. There was a certificate that stated the animal was born in captivity of captive parents, a form that authorized the movement of this member of an endangered species; a U.S. Fish and Wildlife Export form, the Irish import papers, and a health certificate. Finally there were the tamarin's personal records of its life experience. There were seven copies of everything except the personal records, for experience with previous shipments had proven that each official on the way would keep a set for his files. In fact, on one tamarin shipment, the pilot of the aircraft wanted a set of papers, although no one has ever discovered why he wanted them.

No one would argue the value of the Endangered Species Act or the Convention on International Trade in Endangered Species (CITES). These are essential for the protection of the animals that remain in the wild, and even in captivity. But many feel that some exceptions should be made to ease the process for those engaged in captive propagation and other important work for these species' benefit. Some form of official recognition of captive propagation programs might make both funding and the movements of animals a little easier.

The success of the SSPs will hinge on the careful management of that most difficult of all species—*Homo sapiens*. There has always been a degree of rivalry in the zoo world, as in any other profession. On the whole, it is friendly—nothing causes more joy and hilarity than someone else's error, as when the Lincoln Park Zoo prepared a male orangutan for shipment only to have it give birth to a fine baby on the eve of departure, or when the National Zoo acquired a male camel as a stud only to discover he had been castrated. Still, zoos may be critical of each other. There is probably no breeder of *any* kind of animal who has not cast an eye over a colleague's breeding stock and muttered to himself that he would not give house room to that particular creature, or has grumbled, "No wonder he isn't doing well; look at that barn!" Although all accredited AAZPA members must meet certain standards (and these are high), some curators may not want to trade with a given institution. Occasionally, curators have tried to breed for a perfect type, in spite of the fact that there is considerable variation in most wild populations, and may be reluctant to see their beautiful animals mixed with those that seem less perfect.

What is more, there is a people shortage. The number of zoo professionals who have the knowledge of a given species and its management to act as a species coordinator is not great, and all of them are already busy with other work. Serving on committees takes time, and anyone who has ever worked with a committee knows all too well that usually the work is done by two or three people, and that this can be tedious and time consuming.

SSPs have evoked enthusiasm within the profession, and properly presented, have the potential of becoming excellent public relations with a public that is concerned with species preservation. However, some feel that the hazards have been somewhat underestimated. There are those who fear that too many people have stars in their eyes and are moving too fast—albeit on a sound premise—faster than financial and human

The importing of hoofed animals, such as Bactrian camels, that might transmit disease to domestic animals is monitored by the United States Government.

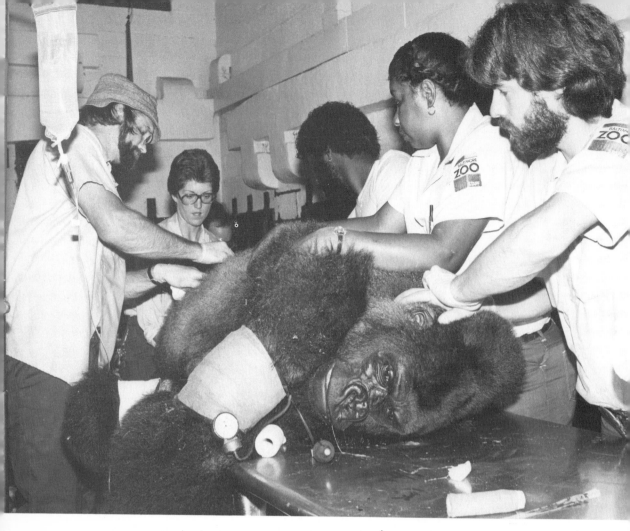

Dr. Mitchell Bush, Head of the Office of Animal Health at the National Zoo, and resident, Dr. Jo Gayle Howard, examine a gorilla prior to its shipment. Baltimore Zoo staff members assist.

resources will allow, and outrunning our knowledge. Although some of the proposed species are already breeding well, others are not at present, and some are unfamiliar. To take one example, some might question if enough is known about Sumatran rhinos, forest animals that browse on twigs and fruit and leaves—they think—to bring a number out of the wild. Such things are being debated within the profession.

The SSPs are a new venture and are no more certain to succeed than any other human enterprise that has never been tried before. No one had ever built an Ark before Noah tried it either. One can just picture him standing there in the drizzle while the bystanders asked how he was going to feed the snakes and why he was bothering to take along a pair of skunks and if he was sure that an Ark was really big enough. And Noah may have replied, "Look boys, the water's up to my knees. Either pick up a hammer or get out of the way."

IT'S ALL A NUMBERS GAME

Until the giant pandas displaced them in public favor, the white tigers ruled supreme as the National Zoo's most famous inhabitants. These rare animals, with their ice-blue eyes and white coats striped with chocolate brown, occur occasionally among Bengal tigers and seem to be most common in the Indian State of Rewa. There the Maharajah of Rewa, fascinated by the beautiful cats, has been breeding them for many years. In 1960, he agreed to present one to the children of the United States, and so Mohini, whose name means Enchantress, arrived at the National Zoo under the personal escort and tender care of Dr. Theodore Reed, who was then the Director.

Mohini and her offspring have fascinated the public, and puzzled them as well. They are so striking that they arouse speculation, and many explanations for white tigers have been heard around the tiger yard. Since, like all tigers, they swim and frolic in the water with uncatlike enthusiasm, some visitors decide that they have been bleached by chlorine in the water. Others guess at sex or age as an explanation for the tiger's coloring, or that they are a special kind of tiger. One visitor was heard explaining to a child that those were zebras.

In the summer of 1982, visitors were treated to a view of tiger domestic life—a white tigress, one of Mohini's granddaughters, taking her ease under a clump of bamboo, eyes half closed as she dozed in the dappled shade. Suddenly, a pair of rowdy cubs erupted from behind the bamboo, swatting at their mother's tail with fat, paddy paws, dashing off again to their play. Back they would tumble to climb on their mother as if she were a convenient rock, chew at her ruff, bite her tail, until she pinned one to the ground with one great foot, growling with mock ferocity. All was what one might expect of a tiger family, except that this white mother had orange cubs.

This proved to offer even more confusion to visitors, one of whom, musing on the subject, asked the guide at the Lion-Tiger Exhibit for an explanation. She responded by asking if he knew anything about genetics.

"I sure do," said the visitor. "My wife had a red-headed baby, and I read up on genes until I was sure everything was O.K. in my family, but I didn't know it would be the same for tigers."

It is the same for tigers—and for elephants and peacocks and rattlesnakes. The laws of heredity apply to us all. The workings of these laws are a central concern of captive propagation, for in addition to trying to preserve part of the world's diversity of species, captive propagation is concerned with preserving diversity *within* species.

No one needs to be told that no two humans are alike (always excepting identical twins), and the same is true of all other living things that, like humans, reproduce sexually. The differences may not always be obvious, but those that know individual animals well can usually tell them apart. Each tiger has a distinct stripe pattern. The giant pandas can be distinguished because, the saying goes, "Ling-Ling wears panty hose and Hsing-Hsing wears knee socks," referring to the height of the black markings on their hind legs. My retriever, a harmless but enthusiastic collector of box turtles, has presented me with as many as five in a morning's walk. All have the typical domed upper shell, and the lower shell that closes tightly to protect the turtle, but each has brown and yellow markings on the shell that are so distinct that I can easily recognize it on a second meeting. Such markings are very useful to field biologists and others who need to recognize animals in the wild.

Diversity, however, goes much deeper and is much more important than simply a matter of recognition. To see why this is so, we must again return to our biology. If the memory of making neat charts of the probable outcome of mating an individual that carries gene combination AaBB with one that has aabB is an unhappy one, bear with me. Genetic considerations are at the root of many changes you may see in the zoo.

An animal's appearance, its physiology, and much of its behavior are determined by the action of genes that are located in a definite sequence along the chromosomes in the nuclei of the cells. Genes may regulate one trait or affect several, or combine to govern some traits. With the exception of the XY pair, the "sex chromosomes," chromosomes occur as like pairs, carrying genes that govern a certain set of the traits that appear in the animal.

Not all genes for a trait issue the same instructions. There is a human gene that orders blue eyes and one that results in brown eyes. There are at least three different human genes for blood type. In all, about twenty per cent or twenty thousand of the approximately one hundred thousand human genes are known to have two or more of these forms. None of us is possessed of one or another form of all twenty thousand, but you and I and the man next door are probably living our lives under the influence of about six thousand seven hundred of them, a different combination for each of us. Allowing for the different numbers of chromosomes in each species, most other vertebrates have roughly the same degree of diversity.

If two genes are different, one is often dominant, and is the one directly expressed. The effects of the recessive gene do not appear directly unless it is carried on both of the chromosome pair (although it may make itself felt indirectly). To use a familiar example, a blue-eyed person marries a brown-eyed person. Brown is dominant and their baby will have brown eyes *unless* the brown-eyed parent had a blue-eyed parent. Then they have a fifty-fifty chance of a blue-eyed baby.

A white tigress plays with her orange cub. She received the gene for white coat from both parents. The cub inherits it only from her and is colored like its orange father.

The *unless* happens because, when the egg and sperm are formed in the parents before fertilization, the germ cells divide. The egg and sperm that will unite in a new individual contain only half the normal number of chromosomes, and the new baby receives half its genes from each parent, in this case a gene for blue eyes from the blue-eyed parent because that is all that is possible, but either a blue-eyed gene or a brown-eyed one from the other parent because he or she carries both. Which combination appears in the child is purely a matter of chance. The parent with both traits is said to be *heterozygous* for eye color, while the blue-eyed parent is said to be *homozygous*.

(This also explains white tigers. The gene for white coat is a rare recessive. Two white tigers will have white cubs, because they carry only the recessive white gene, but mated with one of the usual tiger orange, the cubs will be of the dominant color, orange. *Unless* the orange tiger carries the white gene as well; in that case, the cubs might be of either color.)

These differences originate as mutations, changes in the chemistry of a single gene, or realignment of the genes on a chromosome. Any mention of mutation raises images of the two-headed monster of science fiction, but, in fact, mutations are relatively common. It is true that most mutations are likely to be a disadvantage to the individual in which they occur because they may interfere with the smooth working of a well-balanced system, somewhat like trying to repair a wrist watch with parts from an alarm clock. In spite of that, a fair number of mutations may be neutral in their effects, and a few may have potential value.

Such mutations enter the gene pool and get passed around as animals mate. Each animal has a unique set of genes, and, as each parent contributes half of the genes that will form the new individual, each mating results in a new gene combination, so genes are continually reassorted as they pass to new generations. Ones that have harmful effects often disappear because the individual that receives them does not live to pass them on. Others remain recessive, but spread slowly through the whole species, although remaining less common than their opposite form.

We know that not all genes are equally common. The gene that results in hemophilia is uncommon. So is the gene that results in humans having six fingers or toes instead of five, although a gene with a similar effect is common in cats. There are differences in the frequency of blood types, so that we often hear appeals for donors of the less common types. White tigers are rare and black leopards are less common than spotted ones, although both colors may turn up in the same litter.

Some other genes may be more common in certain regions of the world. Blue eyes are often found in people whose ancestors came from northern Europe. People of Asian descent have a distinctive fold of the eyelids. Sickle-cell anemia is usually found in those whose ancestors came from central Africa.

Individual animals of many species do not travel far in their lifetimes—our remote ancestors lived in isolated groups—and certain gene combinations may become most common among their local populations, the animals that live and breed in one area. This is especially likely to be true if the mutation is useful there, offering a tolerance for heat or cold or resistance to disease. Local populations may become distinct enough to be easily recognized as darker or larger than the species average.

If a local population becomes somewhat isolated for a long period of time—-perhaps by a mountain barrier, or a river, or on an island—the differences may accumulate until it becomes enough unlike its relatives to be called a subspecies. (White tigers, for example, are *not* a subspecies, because their genes are part of the gene pool of Bengal tigers; Siberian tigers and Javan tigers are subspecies because their distinctive combination of traits is only found in those populations.) If the isolation is complete and prolonged, it may become an entirely new species.

And what has all this to do with captive propagation? The answer is that this genetic diversity seems to be a very important characteristic of a species. A certain level of diversity appears to be natural, and individuals that are heterozygous are usually more hardy, healthier, and have more offspring than those that are homozygous.

All of the reasons for this are not clear, but it relates to two things. Harmful genes are usually recessive and uncommon. As long as most individuals carry the dominant form or both forms of the gene, few suffer ill effects. In other cases, there seems to be a genetic compromise. Gene A will be useful to the species under some conditions and gene a under different ones. In some other cases, a recessive gene may be harmful in homozygous form, but helpful in the heterozygous combination. This might be at some stage in the animal's life or relate to certain parts of the environment and the animal's ability to use these. Geneticists argue over why this is so, but the evidence of many studies seems to bear out the belief that a certain level of heterozygosity is important to a species.

The ability to produce different types of individuals offers a species options. It may allow different populations of a species to make use of different habitats, or even enable the same population to use different patches within the same habitat. Some African larks, birds that feed and nest on open ground that is often barren and rocky, appear in several different shades of color—reddish, blackish, or sandy. These colors match the soils where the larks live, and are commonest where most of the soil is of that color. But birds of several colors can be found where the soil forms different colored patches, and the birds seem somehow to "know" where they match and are protected. If disturbed, they will return to the matching patch where they are camouflaged.

The yellow-wattled lapwing, an Indian shorebird that nests on open beaches, has a population that lays reddish, speckled eggs where the beaches are of red sand, while most of the species lay dark eggs that match ordinary soil. Some species of snakes and lizards also make use of two color phases in this way.

Recessive genes, probably hitherto neutral in effect, may offer resistance to a new disease. In the 19th century, homesick colonists introduced a number of European animals to Australia, never stopping to think that these had no natural controls in a new environment. Among these were ordinary European rabbits, harmless, attractive little creatures that the colonists remembered as being pleasant to have about, and as being good to hunt. Once in Australia, the rabbits, free from any hindrance, bred as rabbits can, and before long they were destroying the countryside, leaving no food for the important herds of sheep, or for the native animals.

In an effort to control this plague, the Australians introduced myxomatosis, a disease of South American rabbits. The disease ran like wildfire through the rabbit population, wiping out about ninety-five per cent of the animals in a few years. But five per cent survived. They carried a gene that gave them resistance to the disease so that they either did not get it or recovered. Who knows how long this gene had lain hidden in a species that had never needed it; it might have been carried along for centuries as a recessive. Such a rare gene can save a species.

A third important option to preserve is similar to this. Even if man does not interfere with the environment, it is always changing. Climates change over centuries; lands grow drier or warmer or colder; the plants that grow there change; other animals may put in an appearance. Genetic diversity may give a species options with which to meet these challenges. If an area that has always had enough water slowly begins to dry up— and this is happening in some parts of the world—one of those genes that is essentially neutral in its effects under current conditions, and has ridden along in the population for hundreds of years, uncommon and unnoticed, may endow a few members of a species with the ability to live on what water they can get from their food or from the dew that falls at night. These would then be able to carry their species with them into the future.

The aim of captive propagation is to breed animals in such a way that it will be possible to release them to live wild at some time in the future. This means retaining all the genetic diversity of the wild species with all of the protections and the options for survival that it offers. There are many genetically controlled behaviors that are needed for survival in the wild. A pheasant chick crouches automatically when anything flies over its head; until it learns the difference between a falling leaf and a hawk, it has protection. Attempts to release wild turkey chicks that were the result of crosses with domestic turkeys have failed repeatedly because such chicks seem to carry "foolish genes"—and domestic turkeys are pretty foolish—that make the young birds too trusting or allow them to nest in unsafe places. Chicks that are pure wild turkey have survived, so that wild turkeys are once again found through much of their former range. If animals are to be returned to the wild, they must not only *look* like turkeys or tamarins or tortoises, they must *be* real turkeys or tamarins or tortoises, complete with the traits that enable their species to survive.

But why should this diversity be lost? The genetics of endangered species is often called the genetics of scarcity because it deals with small numbers of animals, whether they are in the wild or in a zoo. And when you deal with small numbers, genetic diversity can easily be lost. In fact, it may not even be there to start with. Remember that not all genes are equally common, nor are they evenly distributed through a species. A small number of animals may not provide a fair sample of their species' diversity.

When there are only a few animals, their offspring can only breed with each other, or with their parents, and thus become inbred. There are mother-son, father-daughter, or brother-sister matings. The offspring of such matings have a substantial proportion of their genes in common, probably one fourth in a brother-sister mating, for these two animals have only one set of grandparents. This means that they will be homozygous for many more traits than animals that are less closely related. When most of the

Efforts to reintroduce the Hawaiian State Bird, the Nene goose, have been somewhat hindered by the occurance of a recessive gene that causes some goslings to have only thin coats of down.

A true wild turkey is wary and wiley. Those crossed with domestic turkeys may carry "foolish" genes and not be capable of surviving in the wild.

members of a population become homozygous for a trait, its alternate form may be lost, with a resulting loss of diversity.

Inbreeding not only results in lost genes, but may sometimes threaten the survival of the colony or even the species. This can happen if the animals become homozygous for harmful traits. Usually, these are recessive, and although they are present and crop up from time to time in the population, are rendered harmless by the presence of the dominant form of the gene. In inbreeding, these harmful recessives have a much greater chance of coming together. Such harmful genes may affect any phase of the animal's development, but they are especially common in traits that concern reproduction, such as those that govern the survival of the young animal or the fertility of the adult, and result in a condition known as inbreeding depression. In an extreme case, there may be so few survivors that the colony dies out.

It was a study of inbreeding, conducted in 1980 by Dr. Katherine Ralls of the Department of Zoological Research at the National Zoo, that forcefully brought home to the zoo community the importance of genetic management. Prior to that time, although several workers had suspected that inbreeding depression was becoming a problem in zoo animals, there was no proof. Inbreeding depression does not affect all species with equal severity. Many zoos had such incomplete records that they were unaware of the degree of inbreeding present in their animals. In practice, the effects of inbreeding can be similar to, and thus masked, by a number of other conditions, such as parasites, poor nutrition, and infections. Only statistical analysis of the records could offer the answer.

Dr. Ralls based her study on a herd of small antelope, known as Dorcas gazelles, that was founded by a pair that President Bourgiba of Tunisia presented to President Eisenhower in 1960. Animal gifts from heads of state such as the giant pandas, the tigress, Mohini, and others usually find homes at the National Zoo, and these two gazelles, known as Granny and Pappy, were duly welcomed into a National Zoo enclosure.

They were a welcome gift, for Dorcas gazelles are delightful animals. Part of their charm is their small size; adults stand only two feet at the shoulder and are often mistaken for babies by visitors who fail to notice their serviceable horns. In spite of their delicate appearance, they are tough little desert animals, well adapted to wresting a living from the harsh environment of their native North Africa. Their tawny, sandy colored coats form an effective camouflage, long legs provided speed for escapes, and they are able to go for days without drinking. In small herds, they travel their arid home, successful in meeting its challenges and seeming unlikely candidates for trouble in captivity.

If you visited the Zoo today, you would find in a grassy enclosure a herd of these graceful creatures, their little tawny bodies dotting the hillside as they lie soaking up the sunshine and chewing their cuds, jaws moving in a dreamy rhythm. On frosty mornings they race uphill and over logs, bounding into the air on stiff legs like Mexican jumping beans, engaging in mock challenges and battles. Calves with floppy ears and busily twitching tails follow their mothers to nurse or test the speed potential of long unsteady legs. If ever there were a sound and healthy group of animals, these appear to be it, but it has not always been that way.

As soon as Granny and Pappy had settled down in their new home, nature began to take its course, and Granny began to produce calves at suitable intervals, an average of one a year. These calves grew up and proceeded to have calves of their own and, until 1965, all seemed well; a few calves died, as is normal and expectable, but most survived and grew. But by 1966, the survival rate began to drop. Some of the females conceived late and were poor mothers. The new babies suffered from pneumonia, from intestinal problems, and from inanition, a condition in which nothing obvious seems to be wrong with the baby but it just lacks energy, even the energy to nurse, and is simply not what farmers used to call thrifty.

The Zoo's veterinarians tackled the problem by various means. The gazelles were moved to another enclosure to try to eliminate the intestinal parasites which are one of the plagues of any zoo. These drain the animals' energy, making them susceptible to infections, and they are very hard to control when herds are living in a confined area. In time, the parasite situation at the zoo improved, but not the calves; all the calves born in 1970 died before they were six months old, and the 1971 and 1972 seasons were very little better. It began to look as if what had been a healthy, thriving herd was headed for extinction.

Then, in 1971–72, several changes occurred. The vets started giving new babies of all hoofed animals a shot of penicillin at birth, as well as treating the unbilical cord. They also discovered that the hay that the zoo had been feeding its herds was deficient in selenium, an important trace mineral that we are beginning to hear a good deal about in relation to human health. New feeds containing selenium and Vitamin E were added to the diets of all hoofed animals. A third change was the arrival of a new male Dorcas gazelle from the Detroit Zoo to replace Pappy and Granny's son Red, who was the current herd sire.

In the following years, the records of the calves turned completely around. Not only did babies once more survive and thrive, the birth rate itself rose, and once more, the Dorcas gazelle herd was in business, producing healthy, frisky babies. In 1976, the herd again moved to new enclosure and another new breeding male came to the Zoo, this time from San Antonio. The problem seemed to be solved.

But what was the problem? Was it infection or parasites or deficient diet or some sort of combination of all of these? Or was it something else, possibly inbreeding depression? Dr. Ralls had been working with records from various zoos of the breeding success—or lack thereof—of several species of hoofed animals. Because the National Zoo had unusually complete records of the breeding and medical history of Granny, Pappy, and their progeny—records of 93 births, which formed a statistically substantial group—this herd offered a prime subject for her study.

The Dorcas gazelle herd was founded by two presumably unrelated animals (presumably, because since they came from the same region and were caught at the same time, they may, in fact, have been related), Granny and Pappy, whose first calves lived and grew up. As the young females matured, they bred with their father, for usually only one male in such a herd breeds, producing inbred calves. Then, from 1970 to 1972, the herd sires were two of Pappy and Granny's sons, so that matings were between full brothers and sisters, or mother and son in Granny's case. In those years, all the calves were inbred and highly so, and only three lived. In 1972, the new male,

The Dorcas gazelles once more produce healthy, frisky calves.

Detroit, and a new, wild-caught female arrived; few inbred calves were born, and mortality dropped. But this was also when the penicillin and selenium treatments were started.

Sitting down to her figures, Dr. Ralls cleared away the confusion. The improved diet and medical practice had indeed improved survival of non-inbred calves, but they had had little, if any, effect on inbred ones. The causes and timing of the deaths were strikingly different, most of the non-inbred calves dying, if they were going to, in their first few days, the inbred ones tending to drag along for weeks with general weakness. More than that, the inbred females conceived later in life and had fewer calves. The study formed the first clear statistical indictment of inbreeding among captive wild animals.

To clinch the matter, Dr. Ralls and her associate, Jonathan Ballou, proceeded to extend the study to other species. They turned to the records of the many centers that keep and raise monkeys and apes for laboratory use, which, since many nations have restricted primate exports, are seriously concerned with successful reproduction among the animals they now own. Although the effects of inbreeding varied somewhat among these species, they were almost always decidedly negative. The same was true for a number of species of small mammals in the National Zoo's collection.

An additional indictment of inbreeding comes from the behavior of the animals themselves. Although inbreeding does take place among wild animals (more among some species than others), most that have been studied seem to avoid it. Mice can apparently detect relatives by scent and will avoid them as mates. Many animals leave home before they reach breeding age; others stay but refuse to mate with a very familiar animal, which would often be a brother or sister. Often only the senior pair in a herd or pack do the breeding, or a male is replaced by a rival before his daughters reach breeding age. Even in captivity, animals may refuse to mate with a long-time companion, even if that one is not related.

Whenever inbreeding is discussed, there is usually someone who raises the issue of the laboratory mice and rats that represent highly inbred lines, deliberately developed so that experiments can be closely controlled. What many people do not realize is that the laboratory animals in these lines are the survivors of many attempts to get such lines established, as many as 19 out of 20 colonies dying out in a few generations from inbreeding depression.

There is no way of telling how many colonies of zoo animals have vanished from their zoos because of inbreeding depression over the years; probably a great many. However, even in populations that must remain small—as inevitably some must in captivity—it now appears that the problem has an answer. Recent work that Alan Templeton of the University of St. Louis has done on a herd of Speke's gazelle at the St. Louis Zoo indicates that it may be possible to breed out inbreeding depression.

Inbreeding does not affect all members of a species with equal severity; some seem to be resistant to the negative effects. Instead of trying to avoid inbreeding, which was impossible, Templeton chose healthy inbred animals as parents for the next generation and paired them so as to increase the genetic variability of the herd by equalizing the representation of the founders' genes. Actually, he was selecting animals that could adapt to a new form of mating system, one that favored inbreeding rather than outbreeding. The result has been a marked decrease in inbreeding depression. The herd has increased rapidly, also an important factor in such management, and is now divided among several zoos.

Such a technique will never be a first choice in captive propagation, but rather an option to be tried when there are only a few captive animals and no more can be obtained from the wild. Inbred animals are genetically different from the wild ones; there is no help for that. That might mean, although it is not certain, that they would have trouble surviving in the wild. Yet, despite the method's drawbacks, it is good to know there is such a way to preserve a species, (even if it is somewhat changed) that might otherwise vanish from our zoos, or, in an extreme case, become extinct.

Another result of Dr. Ralls study was to underline the great importance of records, for obviously, it is impossible to avoid inbreeding or to manage animals for diversity unless someone knows where they came from and who they are related to. The AAZPA now states unequivocally, "No area of professional concern and practice in the long-term management of animal populations is more essential than specimen records. Without continuously and scrupulously maintained records of each individual animal's lineage, fertility, sex, longevity, care and medical history, populations can not be managed to avoid inbreeding and other pathological patterns; long-term preservation will not be possible."

The information furnished by the ISIS system is no better than the information that is received from each zoo. Each zoo must serve its own needs, and there are many effective ways of keeping records, but a look at a typical card from the National Zoo may serve as an example of the sort of detail that might be included.

Under this system, each animal has its Accession Number, which it receives at birth or on its arrival in the Zoo, whether by trade, loan, or from the wild. Even stillbirths are accessioned. Each animal, from elephant to mouse, has a card—now in the same format used for the ISIS records—where its complete biography is recorded, and much of that information is reported to ISIS. So complete is this information, that it results in a complete animal biography—such as that of Anjana, Accession Number 101421.

On December 18, 1975, there was a birth in the Monkey House. This was a lion-tailed macaque, the latest addition to a lively colony of monkeys from India whose name comes from the fact that their tails, like a lion's, end in a tuft of hair. They also sport lion-like gray manes. The new addition, black furred, big eared, and pink faced, was the daughter of Gustav, #29609, the feisty troop male, and Mom, #100244. The keepers recorded her first appearance at 8:00 A.M., when they found her snuggled in her mother's arms, her fur already dry, but the umbilical cord still attached. By January, they were able to sex her, and feeling that she should have a house name that would indicate her Indian origins, they named her Anjana after one of the goddesses of Hindu mythology. When she was a few weeks old, the keepers tattooed the number *21* on her left thigh. Tattoos, leg bands, and ear tags form permanent identifications for animals and those numbers appear on their cards.

Anjana grew rapidly, and by January was climbing alone—"Off her mother"—the first step in monkey independence. In June, she was playing freely with the other young monkeys, but still under her mother's watchful eye, for when she caught her foot in a log, her mother quickly moved to free it. By April of 1978, she was well grown, weighing 3.2 kgs., and by December of that year was learning the skills she would need as an adult, for she was seen carrying her mother's latest infant. In April of 1979, she had her first estrus, the time when females are sexually receptive and fertile, and her own first infant was born the following December.

As of January 1985, Anjana is still alive and healthy, the mother of several youngsters, including a new baby sired by a new and unrelated troop male. But when she does die, hopefully at a ripe old age, her death will be recorded, numbered, and the cause entered on her card. Even the disposition of her carcass will be recorded. Most such carcasses go to the Smithsonian's Museum of Natural History, for exotic animals are of great interest to scientists.

Translated into narrative form, all of this information comes from one specimen card, and indicates the detail that goes into zoo records today; increasingly, these are on computer tape. However they are kept, they are the essential and basic information for animal management.

Although inbreeding is a matter for concern, it is not the only thing to be considered in genetic management, or necessarily the most important. No matter how many animals are present, they all must reproduce themselves or diversity will be lost. Let us say we have a bag of colored balls representing genes. Many of these balls are brown, nearly as many are red, a few are yellow, many fewer are white, and a very few are green. We draw them out by handfuls, representing matings. If we draw one handful, the odds are that we will not draw many, if any, of the less common colors. Draw them all by handfuls, and every color will be represented in at least one draw. If we put them all back in the bag, shake them well, and draw them all repeatedly, a few might become stuck in a seam and lost, but very few. If we do not draw all the balls—or fail to put

Anjana, the lion-tailed macaque, has borne several healthy infants. (Extra paws belong to a third animal in the rear.)

some back—some colors are going to disappear or become very rare. If we read animals and their genes for handfuls of balls, we can see that the genes of non-breeders die with them and are lost to the population.

Further, if we draw a handful, note its colors, and make up several more handfuls of the same colors, then dump them back into the bag, we are going to change the proportions of the original mix substantially. This happens when a few prolific animals do most of the breeding, such as the tiger at the Bronx Zoo, who certainly must be the grand old lady of tigerdom. She has contributed over fifty cubs to the captive tiger population in her day, so that her genes must be coming up on almost every "draw." This results in certain gene combinations from those few prolific individuals appearing more frequently at the expense of those of less fecund animals.

So how are we to avoid this loss? The answer lies in playing the numbers game. This starts with providing enough founders for our captive population. Obviously, one or two pairs will not do, but space in zoos is limited and animals may not be readily available. Luckily, even five pairs of *unrelated* animals can carry ninety per cent of the diversity of their species, and, although more would be better, most authorities accept this as a minimum.

Now we encourage these, by every means possible, to increase rapidly, thus making sure that all gene combinations are well represented. We also make sure that each of the ten founders has an equal representation (draw all those balls). Depending on the species, and its way of mating, and the length of time that the program is expected to have to continue, fifty to five hundred breeding animals will provide a safe margin for diversity. (Five hundred is a lot of animals. This number would be more likely to apply to very long-term programs and to animals that are being managed in the wild.)

These animals would be divided among several zoos, both to protect them if disease should strike one institution, and because subdividing them also protects some of the less common gene combinations. Animals will be traded between institutions from time to time, on a regular schedule, so that genes can travel through the population as they would in the wild. And meticulous records will assure that all of this takes place and that the animals do not become inbred.

Such programs are already in effect and explain why you now see large numbers of one species in one zoo, large numbers of a different species in another, and fewer species in both. The workings of such a program can be found in the history of the Przewalski's horse, or the Mongolian Wild Horse, the only true wild horse remaining in the world. All other so-called wild horses are domestic horses gone wild, although they have often done so with considerable success.

Przewalski's horses are stocky, pony-size animals, sandy yellow with dark stockings and a dark stripe down their backs. Instead of the flowing mane of domestic horses, theirs is stiff and erect, looking as if it had been clipped, and they have no forelocks.

This domestic Mongolian mare (note the long mane and forelock) was bred to a Przewalski's horse stallion in 1906, and bore a fertile hybrid foal.

They bear a strong resemblance to the wild horses that appear in Ice Age cave paintings, and in fact, seem to be very little changed since their appearance in the fossil record of the late Ice Age. But until very recently these ancestors of our horses lived wild in the remote steppes of Central Asia. Although there have been occasional reports of sighting tiny herds, they are almost certainly extinct in the wild; since about 1900, however, these horses have been bred in European zoos. Few of us realize that the animals hunted and portrayed by our Stone Age ancestors lived into historic times, that some are with us today. By luck, and the concern and interest of a few individuals, we still have such animals as European bison and Przewalski's horse as tokens from the past.

All of the known Przewalski's horses living today are the descendants of eleven that were captured around 1900 and one mare that was wild caught in 1947. Breeding centered in Europe, although between 1902 and the 1930s, the Bronx, Philadelphia,

Cincinnati, and the National Zoos all exhibited the horses, bred them, and returned some stock to Europe. After that, breeding in North America stopped, and these lines died out, possibly from lack of interest or lack of space for an animal that looks too much like a domestic one to be an exciting exhibit. In 1956, the Catskill Game Farm, in Catskill, N.Y., imported more Przewalski's horses from Germany and from these, and from a small herd from England that is owned jointly by the National Zoo and the Minnesota Zoo, come the horses in the United States today.

Breeders justly point with pride to the success of the Przewalski's horse, but the Monday morning quarterback can see errors in their past management that now give cause for concern. In 1906, a domestic mare was bred to a Przewalski stallion. Despite the fact that the two species have different chromosome numbers a foal was born and proved fertile, and the genes of the domestic horse have entered the gene pool. Further, prolific animals have been encouraged to be so without too much concern about those that were not, and there has been a good deal of inbreeding. Some breeders, despite evidence that points to considerable variation in the wild animal, have tried to breed to an "ideal" type.

Although twelve founders is a sound foundation, uncoordinated breeding has skewed the distribution of these founders' genes. The history of the horses is well documented by the *International Studbook for Przewalski's Horse,* which was established in Prague in 1956 and is the second oldest studbook for a wild animal. (The oldest is that for the European bison, which was founded in 1923.) Analysis of the pedigree shows that two of the founders have each contributed about twenty-seven per cent of the genetic input of the German-line horses in North America, while some others are not represented at all. The Minnesota/National Zoo herd has a broader foundation, with all founders represented, but it carries the genes of the domestic mare.

Recently, breeders have noticed ominous signs among their herds. Deaths are slightly on the rise and the horses die younger. Births have fallen slightly. There are more animals that seem to be infertile, more abortions, more weak animals. In fact, all of the signs of inbreeding depression are becoming evident, especially in the figures that show a wide gap in the fertility of inbred and non-inbred matings. Equally important, emphasis is shifting from the preservation of a curiosity to the preservation of a wild animal that might be reintroduced into some protected part of its native range in the Soviet Union.

In 1979, the North American breeders got together to address the problem. They agreed to a cooperative program through which they could increase the genetic diversity of their animals and decrease inbreeding. By using a computer to mix and

A Przewalski's horse dreams in the sunshine on a Virginia hillside at the National Zoo's Conservation and Research Center.

match different mares and stallions, the breeders were able to determine how closely inbred the hypothetical foals of these matings would be and how each combination would affect the distribution of each founder's genes. Based on these results, they decided on an initial series of moves, involving seventeen horses.

This meant that a computer printout had to be translated into terms of living animals which, although some are easy-going, are essentially wild. The process involved a profusion of forms to be filled out, filed, and approved. Complex shipping routes for large animals had to be devised, some moves as distant as from the Bronx Zoo to the San Diego Zoo. Three mares were shipped to Prague, and there have been exchanges since then with the Soviet Union. Eleven zoos entered into this, bearing considerable expense and expenditure of time and energy, but the moves were all made expeditiously—and not a horse was injured.

But human actions are not the whole of such plans. Without being anthropomorphic, there is what might be called the point of view of the horses which has a bearing on the outcome. Przewalski's horses live naturally in harems. A stallion gathers a group of mares and provides a strong, year-round defense for them and for their foals. He rules for several years until he is displaced by a younger, stronger male, and during this time the family forms a tight, cohesive unit.

Ideally, this would continue in captivity, and there is a growing emphasis on keeping animals in the most natural groups possible. When they are being transferred, however, this may become difficult. Although stallions are replaced by new males in the wild, and new mares enter a harem, such changes in a captive herd can be disruptive, or even dangerous. Stallions can be dangerous, both to other horses and to keepers. Mares also show a good deal of rivalry and form their own dominance hierarchy. They may exclude a rival or newcomer from mating, or even from feeding, and where in the wild she could go off with another stallion, this mare must now do as best she can on the fringes of the group.

It is possible to separate stallions from the herd, except at breeding time, but this leaves the stallion, once the proud master of his harem, with little to do. Food is at hand, shade, water, every comfort except the exercise of interest and concern for his harem and the companionable hours spent grooming another horse, nose to tail, nibbling gently along back and flank.

This separation may also have an adverse effect on breeding, for the mares' interactions seem to stimulate the stallion's interest. He may have preferences and a single mare may not attract him, or she may be so attractive that he may injure her. Courtship among the horses involves a lot of biting and squealing and flying hoofs. A mare shows no reluctance to deliver a swift right hoof to the jaw if she is not in the mood for dalliance, but the stallion may return with vicious bites to bring her into line. Mares have been killed by stallions. Introducing new horses may set off any of these reactions, which explains why it takes careful handling to make changes in an established herd.

Another consideration is that a stallion may attack his sons as they reach maturity. These youngsters are often called surplus males, but they are only a surplus in terms of the space they occupy and the fact that one stallion can service many mares. Their genes are far from being surplus to the gene pool. Breeders have addressed this problem by setting up a stallion depot at the National Zoo's Conservation and Research Center at Front Royal, Virginia, where these young horses can roam the Virginia hillsides until their services are needed elsewhere. Any breeder can draw on this pool, so most of these horses will have a chance to do their part.

So the zoo numbers game is really a two-part operation. One part, calm and academic and technical, takes place in offices and libraries and cool computer rooms. The other moves to an arena of sweat and shovels, of furred and feathered and scaly protagonists—in fact, to the real world of the zoo, where real animals are induced by their curators and keepers to conduct their mating games according to the numbers.

THE MATING GAME

Anyone not involved in the zoo mating game might wonder why it is that two animals of the same species and the opposite sex who live together year after year still do not reproduce. And it is easy to go from there to the assumption that someone must be doing something wrong. Sometimes it is absolutely correct that someone *is* doing something wrong, though in most cases this is not from negligence, but because there is still a great deal to be learned about the requirements of even some very familiar species. A well-fed, well-housed, properly mated animal ought to be producing babies, but reaching this state means a lot of second guessing on the part of their managers.

We do know that for all members of the animal kingdom, except humans, mating is a sometime thing, often running a poor second to other concerns. In time of drought or famine, or when under pressure from overpopulation or some other kind of stress, many animals simply forget the whole matter. The reproductive behavior that preserves the species comes second to the animal's need to preserve itself. Not only must it find food, often a full-time occupation in the wild, but it has to avoid becoming a meal for someone else, a state of affairs that keeps all but the largest on a constant alert. Courtship and mating offer distractions that are costly in time, energy, and awareness, and few animals can afford to lay down their guard on more than rare occasions. As a result, some sense of security has to come to that animal before mating is possible, and the first step toward this is housing designed to make that animal feel at home.

Volumes could be written about proper housing of animals in the zoo, for it has to take into account the behavioral needs of each kind of animal. Animals tend, as the Nobel Prize–winning zoologist, Konrad Lorenz, has said, to *have* behavior in the same way that they *have* spots or stripes. It is not an arbitrary thing, but the result of a long evolutionary process that reflects their basic ecology. Recognizing this, zoos have begun to replace the lines of concrete boxes of the old-style animal houses with enclosures that may be no larger—this may be relatively unimportant—but are designed to meet the behavioral requirements of each species. Monkeys climb and armadillos dig—the two can actually be housed together—but their needs are very different.

Providing a homelike atmosphere for even one group of small mammals involves a number of considerations. All species of mongooses look somewhat alike, though

Inquisitive dwarf mongooses explore the model termite mound that their keepers designed for their comfort.

varying in size. They are generally long bodied, long nosed, long tailed and short legged. They also have in common a considerable intelligence and an acute degree of curiosity. When Rudyard Kipling wrote of Rikki-tikki-tavi that "the motto of all the mongoose family is 'Run and find out' " he was not far wrong. In the wild, they use up energy and satisfy their inquisitiveness in their quest for food, but in the zoo they need space to run about, a space that must be adjusted to the social system of each species but that must include certain things to keep them alert and interested. Otherwise they are likely to be bored, aggressive, or start the aimless pacing and running that used to be common in zoos.

Tunnels and rocks, roots and stumps are good props, giving them a chance to explore and chase each other as well as to hide. The National Zoo's family of dwarf mongooses inhabit a model termite mound, a replica of the red clay castle-like creations familiar to anyone who has visited East Africa. The virtue of this is not only that it shows the little animals in a natural setting, giving visitors a notion of how such animals live in the wild, but that it offers the mongooses, oblivious to the fact that it is a termite mound, a series of tunnels to explore and a good deal of privacy too.

Most mongooses like to dig, and do best with a floor of sand or wood chips that they can scrabble in. O. Anne E. Rasa, of West Germany, who has studied mongooses extensively, tells of three dwarf mongooses that she had to keep in a wire-floored cage for two months before they could go into a regular enclosure. When they finally moved into their new home with its thick floor covering of wood chips, the three animals did nothing but dig for forty-five minutes until they had all the chips piled into one mountain. They then worked just as busily spreading them back again. Only then, the urge to dig satisfied for the moment, did they begin to explore the other amenities of their cage.

Another mongoose requirement is that they have nest boxes for sleeping, privacy, (both from each other and from the public), and to serve as nests for the babies when they arrive. Many species of mongooses enjoy a warm spot (often supplied by an infrared heater or some such arrangement) over a comfortable lounging ledge, which not only attracts the animals, but allows the public to watch them while they are napping. A few species like water, but most detest dampness, shaking their paws like cats and showing considerable discomfort.

And they need to scent-mark. Scent is one of the most potent communicators among mammals. The dog that trots from pillar to post, sniffing and cocking his leg, is giving and getting information, and the social mongooses make a real ritual of marking sessions, choosing a branch or post that is used by the whole clan. (Some even mark each other, endowing them with a group smell.)

In the old-style menagerie cage in the old-style zoo, everything was scrubbed down frequently, partly for sanitation, partly to control the odors that were admittedly sometimes pretty ripe in small mammal collections. As a result, many animals spent half their time frantically re-marking every surface, once more personalizing their surroundings, for those familiar scents build a sense of security. Curators and keepers now know that scouring an enclosure can be as disturbing to its residents as if they were moved to a wholly new setting. Our sense of smell is so poor in comparison to most other mammals that it is hard to realize how important these signposts are to an animal. It might be roughly compared to rearranging the furniture in a blind person's room, producing complete disorientation. There has to be a nice balance between security and sanitation. All of these considerations have to be met in order to give one group of

A common zebra stallion controls a harem made up of several mares and their foals.

species of small animals the security and homelike atmosphere that will induce them to behave normally and, ultimately, to reproduce their kind.

The proper enclosure has to be inhabited by the right social group; it is not even safe to reason from one species to another closely related one. Many species of mongooses may have similar housing needs, but socially they may be as different as a hermit and a politician. A small Indian mongoose male will probably share a territory with one, perhaps two, females. Egyptain mongooses are essentially solitary. Dwarf mongooses live as a large extended family based on a single breeding pair. Meercats form colonies of several families where the relationships are hard to distinguish. What is right for one species is all wrong for another.

The majority of mammals are polygynous, males mating with a number of females who are able to rear their young with little or no direct help from the father, although males of some species defend their group against predators or defend a territory that females share. It may seem to be a male chauvinist world, but these females do very well indeed; unsuccessful systems do not last long under evolutionary pressures.

There are many permutations of the basic concept of multiple mates, permutations that again reflect the kind of world where that species lives. Common zebras, which are found in grasslands, live like Przewalski's horses in a year-round harem of mares and foals that is fiercely defended by a stallion. Grevy's zebras, whose home is the sub-desert, where food is scarce, spread out; the stallions hold territories while mares and their foals travel alone or form very small herds. A pride of lions is formed by a group of related females who are well able to hunt for themselves and their cubs, but the pride males—who may be brothers—offer some protection and a degree of social stability. A herd of elephants is also composed of females—a self-sufficient and disciplined matriarchy—adult males only form a part of the herd when a female is in estrus. Zoologist Dr. John Eisenberg of the University of Florida lists ten basic polygynous systems in his book, *The Mammalian Radiations*, and although it is not necessary to duplicate these exactly in captivity, the closer the imitation comes to the reality, the greater is the chance of breeding success.

Gorillas, living deep in the rain forest, were known to Western science only from occasional glimpses and local hearsay until 1847, when the first authoritative description reached Europe. This description was purely a physical one, making it clear only that here was a very large and potentially powerful animal, and leaving plenty of scope for the accounts of the beast that explorers of the African forests later sent back. In 1861, the French explorer, Paul de Chaillu, who claimed to be the first white man ever to see a live gorilla, wrote of the animal: "I can vouch that no description can

Despite their size, gorillas are easy-going vegetarians and far removed from the image of King Kong.

exceed the horror of its appearance, the ferocity of its attack or the impish malignity of its nature." This fine set of adjectives has set the tone for the popular impression of gorillas ever since. And then there was King Kong, adding another dimension to the legend. No doubt the first sight of a big male gorilla suddenly emerging from the shrubbery was startling, and a gorilla is possessed of a formidable set of teeth. And, no doubt, the gorillas of these early encounters were in no sweet mood, sensing that these new humans boded no good for gorillas. But they were never King Kongs.

Zoologist George Schaller's 1960 study of mountain gorillas and Dian Fossey's studies from 1967 to 1983 have presented us with a quite different picture of the gorilla. These experts describe an easy-going vegetarian, on the whole rather unemotional, preferring to avoid confrontations, but capable of attack when aroused and fierce in defense of his family. It is still not a familiar image. In zoos, many children greet gorillas by beating their chests and howling, while a number of adults look at them as if they expected to see them carrying off scantily dressed maidens. Gorillas do beat their chests, especially when they are excited, but their interest in maidens, no matter how they are clad, is purest fiction.

Probably in part because of this reputation for ferocity, gorillas have always been popular in zoos. A young female gorilla exhibited in England in 1855 was the first to be seen in Europe, and between then and 1911 some fourteen made their appearances in European and American zoos. All of these were very young animals and all but one, which lived for seven years in Berlin, died within a few months. In 1915, W. T. Hornaday, then Director of the New York Zoological Park, stated, "There is not the slightest reason to hope that an adult gorilla, either male or female, will ever be seen living in a zoological park or garden. . . . We may as well accept that fact—because we cannot do otherwise."

Considering the kind of care that these gorillas received, their poor survival record is hardly surprising. Their caretakers meant well, but no one knew how to feed or house a gorilla and their behavior was a mystery. Many died because, like all primates, gorillas are subject to human respiratory ailments and intestinal problems, and the young animals soon succumbed to pneumonia or disgestive disorders. It is significant that the one gorilla that lived for seven years was separated from the public by glass, as most are today.

These early captives were also fed all sorts of foods that might have suited a human palate, but that made a poor diet for an ape. Mashed potatoes and gravy, ice cream, and roast beef were among the menu items, and one gorilla in a German zoo feasted on beer and sausage, hardly proper for a vegetarian. (However, most zoo gorillas today do receive a small ration of meat and seem to benefit from it.) Even when their diet was more nearly what it should be, most received a great deal of fruit, which forms only a small part of a gorilla's normal diet. None of this should be surprising. The science of nutrition, as applied to exotic animals, simply did not exist then. Indeed, even for domestic animals, and for humans, it was extremely rudimentary.

Another major factor in the gorilla's poor survival rate was an almost complete lack of knowledge about their behavior. Gorillas are social beasts, and yet despite early reports that are full of accounts of the affectionate, cuddly, playful nature of baby gorillas, their social needs seem rarely to have been considered important in their care. In fact, the babies were usually captured by killing their mothers, which was hardly a favorable start. Both their early need for close physical contact and their general need for companions were ignored. Surely, that isolation must have been a factor in their early deaths. If zoo people had communicated then as they do now, someone might have put two and two together sooner than they did, but the days of conferences and publications and papers were still in the future.

Boy (right) meets girl. By patient, careful management, gorillas can be introduced to normal social groups.

In spite of Hornaday's gloomy forecast, a few zoos persisted in trying to keep gorillas, and gradually understanding of their needs did grow. Once they were fed a proper diet and housed under better conditions (although for many years ape cages resembled tiled lavatories) adult gorillas did begin to appear in zoos. Breeding was another story, partly because many of the valuable animals were kept as solitary specimens, including Gargantua, Bushman, and many other famous apes of the 1930s. Bushman was never bred for fear that he might be injured in an encounter with a prospective mate. Gargantua was provided with a mate by his exhibitors, Ringling Brothers, but the new female would have nothing to do with the big ape, thus foiling plans for a "wedding" complete with plenty of media hype.

But even when gorillas were kept as pairs, there were no babies until 1956, when Colo was born at the Columbus Zoo. This exciting first birth was followed by several at the Basel Zoo in Switzerland, including the first gorilla to be reared by his own mother, and then one at the National Zoo. Slowly (the first gorilla birth in England was not until 1971), the number of captive-born gorillas has increased. As of 1985, there are about 550 gorillas in zoos and primate centers around the world, and they are producing about twenty babies a year.

Much of this success in breeding captive gorillas is the result of new information about the behavior of wild gorillas. However, much, in fact most, of our information is based on the field studies of mountain gorillas, while those in American zoos are lowland gorillas. Experts feel that the behavior of the mountain gorilla may be very similar to that of the lowland gorilla, but we also know that different habitats can make quite significant differences in the behavior of animals of the same species. For this reason, there is a little uncertainty on this count. However, these studies are all that there is to go on.

Gorillas are polygynous. A male gorilla's strategy is to attract a number of females and to breed with them, offering them and their offspring protection and territorial defense and cohesion as a group, but taking little part in the care of his babies. Such a male will be a "silver back," a mature male named for the silvery gray fur that appears on his back when he is around thirteen years old. Often there are one or two other adult males in the troop, and younger, black-backed males, as well as females and various youngsters. The youngsters grow up surrounded by playmates and relatives, knowing their place in the group, learning by observation and experience much of the behavior they will need as adults. Both males and females may leave the group when they approach puberty, females often joining another group, while males may travel alone or join other males until they can acquire a harem of their own.

Portrait of Mwasi. Gorillas are distinctive both facially and behaviorally.

The trend in gorilla management now is to try to set up groups that will be as close to the wild social situation as possible, though this is very much easier said than done. The problems lie in the very nature of the gorilla as a social animal and as an individual. They are intelligent, they are also individualistic. Facially, gorillas are quite distinct and it is not hard to recognize individuals by their looks. Further, they might be said to have distinct personalities and show likes and dislikes for other animals which, possibly, in the wild animals have roots in lines of kinship. It is probably incorrect to say that any animal "likes" in the sense that we do. Affinities are more likely based upon relationships and upon a reading of another animal's behavior; still, because of the gorilla's high level of intelligence, it would not be surprising to find that gorillas go a little further than this.

As a result, when adult apes are introduced, instead of falling on each other's necks with delight, females may attack other females and males may bully or tease the females. And bullying or teasing from a 350-pound gorilla cannot be taken lightly. Even if they are willing to share an enclosure, they may show complete disinterest in each other, sitting in different corners and staring in different directions, not a very likely basis for a lively social life. It is easiest to form a group with young animals that are not set in their ways.

Another problem that may arise among many primates during group formation, or the introduction of a new animal to a troop, is a social disruption and realignment of the members, which can end in the death or injury of some members, and of infants. Males are normally tolerant of the youngsters in their own group, but reports from the wild show that when, as happens sporadically, a new male or males takes over the leadership, babies and juveniles sometimes vanish. One theory holds that a male is, innately, only interested in extending his protection to his own, known offspring, and that by killing unrelated infants he brings the females into estrus, mates with them, and assures that his own young get the best of the available resources. Another theory relates the attacks to the stress caused by overpopulation. Whatever its cause, this kind of behavior has been reported for several species of monkeys, and Dian Fossey reported it of her mountain gorillas. In England, the Jersey Zoo's breeding male gorilla, Jambo, also dispatched a baby that was his own but which he had never seen before, and various zoos have reported the same behavior among some of their monkeys. Here is another important factor to be confronted and dealt with in forming groups.

(Such infanticide is not confined to primates. A Prezewalski's horse stallion at the San Diego Wild Animal Park killed a foal, although he had calmly watched the birth and growth of forty-eight other foals. This foal's mother was a mare from the Soviet Union that had been bred to a stallion there before shipment. No one knows how this stallion could have known that he was not the father of that particular foal, but he has since accepted another foal that he sired with the same mare, which gives credence to the theory that he did know.)

Some difficulties with gorillas are the result of captive rearing. Because many adult gorillas now in zoos have spent much of their lives more or less isolated from others of their kind, having been hand reared (either because they came from the wild as youngsters or because their mothers would not care for them), they have never had the chance to learn proper gorilla conduct. This includes mating behavior and the care of babies, things they would have learned from group life in the wild. It is hard to compensate for this lack in fully adult animals that may have acquired a set of psychological hangups that would drive a psychiatrist wild, including such stereotyped behaviors as rocking themselves, pulling out their hair, or shuffling and pacing aimlessly about.

Hand rearing becomes one of those self-perpetuating things, hand-reared mothers producing infants that must be hand reared in turn. However, if they have several births, even hand-reared gorillas may figure out what it takes to be a good mother. Unfortunately, not many captive mothers have had such a record. Gorilla births are still not frequent enough to give most this kind of practice. The Jersey Zoo has a notable record of gorilla breeding, with each of their two females having borne five young. But though they both improved their performance as mothers with each baby, it was not until the fourth births that they were willing and able to care for the infants themselves.

Inexperienced mother apes do not usually abuse their infants, although this may occasionally happen. More often they will clean the baby after birth, carry it for a bit, and then lay it aside as if they felt that this was all that motherhood required. Other ape mothers carry the baby tenderly, but upside down or in a position where it cannot nurse. When such inadequate mothering continues for a day or more, a curator is placed in a very difficult position. Here he has an animal of a rare and endangered species, one with great monetary value and great public appeal. If he pulls the baby for hand rearing, he runs the risk that it will grow up as something that can be exhibited under a sigh saying "gorilla" but that has no more of the social attributes of a real gorilla than a hedgehog. On the other hand, if the infant stays with the mother and dies, he is open to public and possibly some professional criticism. Today there is a growing trend toward waiting as long as possible and toward trying to teach the mother her proper role. Still, this may not be an option. A compromise solution is to take the baby for hand rearing, but to place it with another little ape—even one of a different species—as soon as possible.

Captive groups can rarely be completely natural; it would probably always be difficult to mix a juvenile male with an adult silver back in a captive setting unless he had grown up there, although field studies indicate that a wild male may be very tolerant of a growing son. And a breeding group may need more than one male. Stereotypes aside, male gorillas do not seem to be highly sexed; often it is the females who solicit their attention. Information from the field indicates that males in groups that include another male show much more interest in the females than those who rule alone. These males may need the presence of a possible rival if they are to form certain hormones and build these to the proper levels. Females, in turn, seem to be aware of these levels of male hormones, probably by scent, and show little response to males with low levels.

Evidence supporting this need for a rival surfaced at the National Zoo when the gorillas were moved to a new building designed just for the great apes. In their new home, they had much more space with more interesting features, such as climbing equipment, outdoor yards, a view of other gorillas. After the move a male, who was a proven breeder but had for some time totally ignored all his females, developed a new interest in life and the ladies. While he did not actually share an enclosure with another male, because of the design of the new house he was able to see, hear, and smell the potential rival.

Yet in their annual physicals before the move, the tests indicated that this particular male was sterile, for all practical purposes—not an uncommon state of affairs in captive male gorillas. What's more, the females' ovaries appeared to be atrophied. A year later, the male's semen quality, although still nothing wonderful, had improved and the females had shown appreciable changes for the better. This possibly indicates some connection with their housing and grouping, which included the arrival of two new gorillas. They are not a sociable bunch as yet, and there have been no babies, but there have been matings and the prospects are clearly better than before. Gorillas are now on the move, traveling around the country on breeding loans, and although group formation can take months, or even years, there are fewer single animals, or pairs kept as singles, to be found today.

Another benefit of social groups is that gorillas may begin to show their true colors as handsome, active, intelligent animals instead of the morose, depressing beasts that have been all too common when housed alone. Indeed, in view of gorillas' poor adjustment to captive life, many people—even within the profession—question the morality of keeping these animals, with their proven intellectual capacity, in captivity. Usually these same people dispel their own doubts: As conditions now stand in the wild, it is only in captivity that gorillas and orangutans are likely to survive.

If gorillas have been difficult, many of the hoofed animals have done well in zoos. A survey conducted in 1978 showed that twenty-six species of rare mammals could be considered to have self-sustaining zoo populations. Of these, fifteen were hoofed animals—horses, deer, bison, and antelopes. (Another eight were members of the dog or cat families.) Many of these species follow the ancestral mating systems of many of our domestic animals and respond well to techniques that have been carried over from the husbandry of cows and horses.

With such a history of successful breeding, it would seem that there was little need to worry about the future of these species, and to some extent this is true. But there are

A Pere David's deer hind nurtures her spotted fawn.

growing fears about captive-bred animals—that their care has been too domestic, too unlike the natural behavior of that species to preserve them as a truly wild form. Quieting some of these concerns is the evidence of the wisent, the European bison, which quickly reverted to natural behavior when they were released in a game preserve to live wild, as they naturally returned to their former birth seasons and herd structure. Still, any evidence of change concerns managers.

In general, deer, antelopes, and horses are polygynous, with males either following and mating with one female after another during the season, collecting seasonal harems, or gathering and defending a harem year-round.

One of the most famous and often cited examples of successful captive breeding is the Père David's deer, a species of large deer native to China with the somewhat unusual appearance that led the Chinese to name them the Four Dissimilarities. To the Chinese, they have the horns of a stag, the neck of the camel, the hooves of a cow, and the tail of a donkey. Although their greatest admirers have to admit that they are not the most beautiful of deer, this description is something of a libel, for a big stag is a handsome animal. For over 2000 years they have lived in hunting parks or in zoos. These deer became extinct as wild, free-living animals somewhere about 1122 B.C. By 1900, the only surviving deer, except for a few that had been sent to European zoos, were confined to the Imperial Hunting Park near Peking, where they lived in a semi-wild state, but after the Boxer Rebellion in that year, these deer fell victims to starving peasants and trigger-happy soldiers. After this, in England, the Duke of Bedford acted to gather the sixteen or so animals from the various European zoos into one herd at his estate, Woburn Abbey. The present captive population is the result. In spite of its many vicissitudes, the Père David's deer is still in business.

The herd at Woburn Abbey still exists, living in a semi-wild environment where, for the greater part of the year, their life is placid and untroubled. There, they graze peacefully or soak in lakeside shallows, which they seem to enjoy and which, taken with the evidence of their big, flat hooves, indicates that their ancestors probably lived in marshes. In the spring the herd grazes together, with stags and hinds forming a rough ring around the spring crop of frisky, spotted fawns. Hinds tend to herd together on a basis of relationship and familiarity, mothers and daughters, aunts or cousins usually preferring to stay together.

As the mating season, or the rut, approaches, action steps up. The stags begin to challenge each other, sparring with their antlers, threatening each other, roaring. Their necks thicken and they grow impressive ruffs. They wallow in mud holes until they are well coated; they scrape up great bunches of grass that they carry on their antlers, forming strange headdresses, actions that seem designed to make each stag look as big and impressive as possible.

Two stags will walk parallel to each other with a peculiar rolling, threatening walk, and now, if they are allowed to, sparring matches may develop into full-blown fights. Stags seem to have a good eye for the fighting potential of a challenger and often turn away when they are clearly outclassed, but well-matched pairs may charge and lock antlers, each trying to force the other to his knees. At this point, keepers pay close attention to the proceedings for, occasionally, stags are injured in these fights.

Gradually, males establish a dominance ranking that may change from year to year, or even during the season. This is headed by animals in the prime of life—four or five years old—followed by older and then younger animals. Yearlings and two year olds

A Pere David's deer stag is a majestic animal.

are rarely taken seriously by their elders and often continue to feed with the hinds, although male two years olds may try to sneak in a mating when the harem master is looking the other way. The dominant stag, or stags, herd together as many hinds as possible, often on a patch of ground that the hinds seem to favor, and now spend their time heading off wandering hinds and chasing away rival stags. As the hinds come into estrus, the stag tests each one by scent to judge her condition, curling his lip in the odd, sneering expression known as Flehmen. When he senses that a hind is close to the peak of estrus, he tends her closely until he breeds her.

This is an exhausting season for the stags. No longer can they feed and chew their cuds in peace; in fact, they take little time to eat or rest. As the season progresses, the dominant stags become steadily thinner and more weary, less able to meet the challenges of their rivals. They may be replaced by fresher males lower in the dominance order, so that several stags actually may take part in breeding before the season is finally over. After six weeks or so, most of the hinds are impregnated and leave the stags to go their way. Soon after this, the stags drop their antlers and return to quietly chewing their cuds and taking mud baths, while the eternal cycle begins anew.

What happens to this pattern when it is transferred to a zoo enclosure? Such behavior can be allowed to follow its natural form with minimal interference in Woburn Abbey's four thousand acres, and can be approximated in a place such as the Front Royal Conservation and Research Center, where there is a substantial herd. However, it is difficult to keep truly natural herds in the average zoo. Animals such as these need space, though not necessarily a vast amount in which to run. They do need exercise but, in the wild, they do not gallop around simply for entertainment. A herd flying across the plains is likely to be fleeing for its life, not doing it for fun. Actually, very large enclosures can make it hard for keepers to make sure that every animal is healthy, that it is not being nosed away from the manager at feeding time, that the young ones are not bullied by the elders.

Still, they do need more room than other species and most zoos use about a third of their animal space for the hoofed animals. Not only are these large to begin with, but more than most animals, they like to keep a reasonable distance from familiar keepers and even more from strangers. This is their flight distance, the space that they sense they need for a head start when making an escape. It decreases in captivity but never disappears, and without a good deal of elbow room such animals seem uncomfortable and become very spooky and nervous. Their brains seem to be entirely in their feet, something that makes sense for a prey animal but that may send them crashing into fences or into each other in a small area.

In addition, if two or more males are confined with the females in a relatively small space, the results can be tragic. In a battle for dominance, the loser must be able to remove himself far and fast if he is to escape injury; if he is cornered, he may be gored.

And while the two are charging about, or when a stag is in hot pursuit of a hind, the two become blind to everything else, often running down fawns and crashing into fences, risking broken legs or necks.

The traditional solution has been to keep these species in male-female pairs or as a group of a single male with several females, or to keep the males completely apart. Since hoofed stock have generally been good breeders, the traditional system has worked well. Among most of these animals, there is little difficulty in rotating males, at least as far as the females are concerned. The relationship is rather a casual one. It is probably an advantage for a female to mate with the biggest and strongest male around, but after mating she and her baby can do nicely without him. One male breeds this season and then goes off to another zoo; another one appears next year and the females seem to accept this with a shrug. The difficulties appear with the males.

It appears that at least a few males should be allowed to settle their affairs in the natural way, both for the stimulus that this provides—for the battle may add impetus to the breeding—and to avoid artificial selection by their managers. Stags and bucks may become very aggressive during the rut, and even animals that would feed from the keeper's hand yesterday may threaten him today. As a result, keepers and curators, not unreasonably, may favor the milder animal that is easier to handle; in the wild, however, this might be the very one that would lose out in a battle for dominance. Even if he is fit and in the prime of life, he may lack the assertive qualities that would make him the best sire for the new generation.

Selection by easy handling may also, thus be selection for tameness, a disadvantage for any species that might someday be returned to a wild existence. However appealing and moving it may be to us to have a wild animal approach us with trust, such behavior can only place that animal's life in danger, and any animal that is to live free must keep its wild responses. On the other hand, tameness might well be an advantage to animals that are to be kept in captivity. Selection in either direction should be made intentionally, not as a side effect of management, though if space allows it, natural selection seems the wiser course.

In addition, some breeders have found that the tame stag is a poor breeder. At both the Whipsnade Zoo, the Zoological Society of London's spacious and beautiful zoo in the Bedfordshire countryside, and at the Bronx Zoo, there were stags that became extremely aggressive and a real danger to both keepers and the other males. They were therefore penned up, and a milder stag was allowed to do the breeding that year. In the spring, there were no fawns. The next season a shift gate was installed that allowed the keepers to handle the dominant animal without needing to come close to him, and the next spring saw spotted fawns as before. As with gorillas, there seem to be complicated interactions between animals that govern hormone production and may cause breeding failures when man takes over from nature. Continuing success with these species means finding places outside the conventional zoo setting where they can live more natural lives.

By this time it should be abundantly clear that when we speak of the diversity of nature, we are talking of something more complex than that a giraffe looks different from an elephant. Among other things, we are finding that, although most mammals follow polygynous mating systems, many do so only in a technical sense, and some do not do so at all.

Rufous elephant shrews are not the kind of animals that bring visitors flocking to the zoo. In fact, it is very easy to overlook them completely, for they are small and their enclosure often seems to be empty. Careful scrutiny, like searching a puzzle picture, finally uncovers a small, plump animal crouched under a cactus. A further search reveals another resting three feet away under a rock. At first glance, they seem rather like mice of some sort, but they are not rodents, but members of a family of African animals made up of some fifteen species. They are attractive little beasts with large ears and big, bright eyes, and—the most distinctive thing about them—long, flexible noses. These, like tiny abbreviated elephant's trunks, whiffle and waver to catch passing scents; although, unlike an elephant's wonderful proboscis, they have no ability to grasp, these noses give the little animals their name.

Elephant shrews have never been common in zoos, although they have considerable charm and can be a delightful exhibit. They have had the reputation of being delicate and difficult to keep and births have been rare. Even in Africa they are only common in certain localities and are rather retiring, so on one knew very much about their life in the wild until zoologist Galen Rathbun conducted a field study a few years ago. Rathbun found that, although elephant shrews almost always seem to be alone, they really live as pairs—very independent pairs, but pairs.

Their home is in rather dry, rocky grasslands where, ears on the alert for the least rustle in the leaves, they nose and snuffle through the ground litter looking for small insects, ants, and termites. Each pair of animals claims a territory, which it defends aggressively against all other elephant shrews, males taking the initiative against male intruders while females deal with marauding females. The males maintain a carefully tended trail system through their territories, making it their business in life, by brushing with busy forepaws, to clear every bit of leaf or twig from the internal communication lines that lead to safety and shelter. That they will also maintain their trails in a proper exhibit enclosure is part of their charm as exhibit animals.

The attachment between the two animals may be to the territory rather than to each other, but the effect is that of a monogamous pair that form a lifelong union. And simple liking for a location may not be the whole story either, for when Rathbun started setting up pairs of captive animals, some firmly refused to have anything to do with the mate he selected for them, but did accept another.

A long flexible nose is the trademark of a rufous elephant shrew.

Armed with this new information on elephant shrew mating systems, Rathbun felt that it was worth another try at establishing them in captivity and sent off a founding group to Washington. To protect their delicate noses on the journey, he placed each little animal in a cloth bag and supplied it with several locusts as provisions for the trip. He then fastened the bags with the elephant shrews inside a large basket for their twenty-four hour trans-atlantic flight.

The elephant shrews traveled well, but once they arrived in the zoo, Rathbun was faced with the problem of housing animals that need to be together, but that seem to spend their time in avoiding each other's company, and that need a lot of elbow room. If they are crowded they may be slow to breed—if they do so at all—fight, bite each other's tails, or turn on their young. So he formed pairs of animals, choosing ones that had been trapped at some distance from each other so that they were unlikely to be related, and placed each pair in a large cage with a partial partition down the center and individual shelters so that the elephant shrews could meet, or remain alone, at their pleasure. He also provided them with as much privacy from human disturbance as possible, for they are shy little things, racing away from danger almost as little antelopes might. Wood chips on the floor gave them material with which to build trails. Soon the little animals began to settle down, to build their trails and start to scamper around when feeding time arrived, waiting for their daily rations of grated carrots and apples, sweet potatoes and kale, chopped meat, grated egg yolk, diluted condensed milk, and meal worms, or two live crickets each. And after a few months in their new home, babies began to appear.

The rufous elephant shrew colony has passed through several generations since that time. A large number of babies have been born, for elephant shrews often have twins, precocious, bright eyed, fully furred, and very substantial in size compared to their mother. By the time they are fifty days or so old, they have reached adult weight and are probably sexually mature, old enough to become intruders in the family territory and to be driven off by the parents. In fact, Rathbun found that the young animals could be taken from their parents as early as seventeen days after their birth.

Although the bond between elephant shrews may seem to be something of a marriage of convenience, it is a genuine bond and lasts for life. Probably the earlier failures to breed rufous elephant shrews on a sustained basis were the result of not knowing that here was a species whose members needed to be together without togetherness. Without the initial study of the species in the wild, the rufous elephant shrews would probably have never been successful in captivity, and the fact that other species of elephant shrews have not done as well means that there is still much to learn.

Field studies form the backbone of captive breeding programs, so that curators manage their animals with one eye on reports from the wild and the other on the zoo. Nearly every field study ultimately has some effect on the captive management of that creature as well as on its management in the wild. But if field studies are the backbone, captive observation provides the flesh. The zoo is an ideal laboratory for learning more about a particular kind of creature. By shifting animals around in different combinations, waiting for individual reactions to these —which, if the animals do not care for the arrangements, may be swift and emphatic—by simply watching different animals and recording their actions over a period of time, little details build up a picture that has far more validity than mere anecdote. We know that rufous elephant shrews do not build nests for the babies, but that while they are very small, the mother may carry them from one place to another in her mouth. We know that she nurses them for only a short time, and that she may have another litter only two months after the first. We know that the animals wash their faces with their forepaws. All of these things serve to improve their care and clarify their taxonomic relationships. Possibly most important, we know that it is possible to breed and maintain a colony of a formerly "delicate and difficult" animal, once we understand them.

Monogamous mating systems are also rooted in a species' evolutionary history and its ecology. The road to fitness, in the Darwinian sense of "survival of the fittest," is built on offspring that live to breed in their turn, or to put it another way, in becoming a parent and grandparent as often as possible. It has made sense in his evolutionary history for a male rufous elephant shrew to stake a territory that supplies his needs, and incidentally those of his mate and their young (for as long as they remain with their parents), but in a world of sparse resources there is only room for one female in such a territory. It has also made evolutionary sense for a male golden lion tamarin to help to rear his twins. A female golden lion tamarin might be able to do it alone but the odds are against it, and if she can get help from her older offspring as well, so much the better. For male tamarins and elephant shrews prudence dictates that instead of playing the field and mating with many females, they stay with one and, in one way or another, help to raise the family. These evolutionary imperatives are built into each species and can not be ignored in captivity. It is not that the animal won't change; it can't!

A major problem in the management of monogamous mammals has been in not knowing that they *were* monogamous. It is not always easy to recognize these systems either in the field or in the zoo. A gibbon family of mother, father, baby, and sometimes an older juvenile is so clearly what we think a model family should be that we feel a delighted sense of identity as we watch them. But elephant shrews could be taken for loners—as in a sense they are—and although a pack of wolves or African wild dogs is clearly a social arrangement of some kind, the mass of waving tails and furry bodies may bear more resemblance to a pep rally than a family. But all of these are monogamous systems.

Whatever the numbers of the pack or troop—a wild dog pack may run fifteen or better—its basis is a single bonded pair. Unlike many polygynous systems, where several females may rear their young together, and where a few may even show concern for another's offspring, females in these systems brook no rivals. Elephant shrews and dik diks, tiny African antelopes, drive the youngsters from the home territory as soon as they are old enough. Wolves and wild dogs, dwarf mongooses and tamarins allow them to stay as helpers with the next litter. But as long as they remain part of the pack or troop, neither these youngsters, nor any other adult, will have a chance to breed. Females may never exhibit a normal estrus cycle in the presence of a dominant female, or the dominant female may fight any other that attempts to mate. Dog breeders will testify that female fights can be far more vicious than those of males. The presence of the dominant female may produce such stress that the subordinate one aborts or neglects the infant.

Some readers may remember *Solo* by Jane Goodall and Hugo Van Lawick, an account of an African wild dog pup who was the only survivor of a litter that a subordinate female tried to rear in her home pack. The dominant female harassed Solo's mother and her pups so severely that all the others were killed or died of stress and neglect. We don't like to think of animals, especially mammals, practicing infanticide, but one pack can rear only one litter and this behavior assures that some pups will survive.

Any zoo engaged with programs for these monogamous species has to face the fact that only one female per group will breed, do what anyone may. This means relying on a number of groups, for relying on only one can be risky since the death of one animal will lead to an end of the whole reproductive effort. As a result, the visitor today may find pairs of dik diks or tamarins or gibbons dotted here and there about a zoo, a sight that may, instead of becoming monotonous, offer a view of their family life at different stages, showing babies, young pairs, and growing families.

Today the zoo visitor may also find some animals living a solitary life, a single animal with a large enclosure to itself. A common question is "Aren't they lonely?" In the modern zoo, the answer is usually no, for these are essentially loners. Mating is a passing interlude and their only real social contact is that of the mother with her young. These animals have such short and tenuous mating relationships that they are truly ships that pass in the night, and their relationships are sometimes termed promiscuous. While this term is somewhat out of favor, as such a system can also be considered loosely polygynous and implies a moral judgment that has no place among animals, it is still useful in describing their mating habits.

Among these solitary species is the cheetah, beautiful, graceful, holder of the mammalian record for speed over a short course, seemingly self-contained and self-sufficient. Nearly every field worker has remarked on the cheetha's air of remoteness, its aloof bearing. Joy Adamson even named her book about her cheetah *The Spotted Sphinx*. George Schaller refers to it as "the gentle, elegant cat" and added, "They have reached a peak of evolutionary efficiency in their hunting. Then why are they so sparse, why is the species balanced so delicately between security and extinction? Their refusal to breed in captivity puzzles me too. Thousands of cheetah have been kept in zoos and by Eastern potentates who trained them to hunt antelope, yet only about a dozen births have been recorded. Looking into their haunting eyes, I am aware that the cheetah remains an enigma."

Since 1966, when Schaller made his study in the Serengeti, cheetah breeding has improved and they are somewhat less of an enigma, but the beautiful cats still pose

Dik diks, one of the smallest antelopes, live in monogamous pairs. A hand-reared youngster stands nose to nose with Jo Ann Grumm, Hand Rearing Coordinator for the Friends of the National Zoo.

problems and raise questions. In the wild, cheetahs are almost always found alone; groups are usually a mother with cubs, or males, who may be brothers, who hunt together. Cheetah cubs stay with their mother until they are fifteen to eighteen months old, learning to hunt and support themselves. After they leave their mother, female cubs may hunt together for a time, but soon part company, each finding a place where she can establish herself.

Many of the big cats are somewhat similar in their habits and still breed well in captivity, but the cheetah is in this, as in many other things, an exception. Although Akbar the Great, the Mogul Emperor of India, is supposed to have kept 1,000 cheetahs, allowing them free run of his gardens in the hopes that they would bear cubs, only one litter resulted. And the first cheetah captive birth of modern times took place in the Philadelphia Zoo in 1956.

The reason seems to be that the cheetah disdains the familiar companion. They can be kept as pairs and will live contentedly together, but the relationship remains purely platonic. Whether this reflects some mechanism that works to prevent inbreeding in wild animals, or a version of the "familiarity breeds contempt" syndrome found in other animals, or something peculiar to cheetahs is hard to say, but the practical result is that in order to breed cheetahs, they must be kept from sight and sound of each other.

In South Africa, at the De Wildt Cheetah Breeding and Research Center of the Pretoria Zoo, females live in yards of about an acre each, while males live behind a hill at the far end of the facility. A group of males may be allowed to roam in the "No Man's Land" between the camps, and periodically, a single male is introduced into the run between the female enclosures. He is called a "teaser" or "marker" and is not necessarily the male to do the breeding. However, he quickly locates any female that is approaching estrus, and if the female reacts to his presence, running up and down the fence and rolling like an overgrown kitten, a breeding male, selected for his known fertility, is allowed to enter her enclosure. Copulation may take place at once.

Using this technique, the De Wildt Center has been very successful in breeding the cheetah. Between 1975 and 1979, 128 cubs were born. The Whipsnade Zoo has been another very successful breeder, with several full second-generation births. Some other zoos, using similar methods, have also done well with this graceful cat.

Although not many species of zoo animals are such determined loners as the cheetah, there are a fair number that are basically solitary and considered prudent to house separately. But meet they must if there are to be babies, and not only just time for mating, but for some, a prolonged period of learning and courtship. In 1968, the National Zoo began to introduce a pair of Indian rhinos, Tarun, a male of somewhat unpredictable temper, and Raji, a hand-reared and usually easy-going female. It was four years before these two finally achieved copulation. The courtship of a couple of two-ton animals within a confined space is something to conjure with, and so the two

The cheetah, the "gentle, elegant cat," poses many questions to zoologists.

were only introduced when Raji seemed to be receptive, and then only during the day, when someone could be on watch so that their meeting should not get out of hand.

At these meetings, there was sometimes no action at all, but at other times, the female would approach her mate and rub against him, sometimes standing nose to nose, snorting and honking, even biting his forehead. This might start a wild chase around the yard, arousing fears that the male might get carried away and injure the female or crash into something. However, Taran worked off his surplus energy by attacking other objects, charging a wall, rubbing his horn and his head against it, setting up a thunder that seemed to shake the building. At times, both animals became completely exhausted and broke off their action. Before attempting to copulate, Taran would "dance," a strange, and rather touching, exhibition for so ponderous an animal, lifting his forefeet from the ground, tossing his head, wheeling left and right.

But after three years of such sessions, the two had got no further with their relationship. Finally, the staff decided that at Raji's next estrus, using volunteers to record the action and keep an eye on the proceedings, they would leave the pair together for a full twenty-four hours, except for a two hour feeding break. This would, it was hoped, give them time to synchronize their behavior. It appears that male Indian rhinos need time to learn what they are about. For about six weeks, they remained together, and then, without any fuss or bother, seemingly knowing within themselves that the moment had come, walked out one morning into a fall rain and accomplished their mating. About sixteen months later, the first Indian rhino calf to be born in the Western hemisphere made his appearance; he was named Patrick in honor of Senator Patrick Moynihan, the ambassador to India.

It was only in retrospect that the observers could detect the subtle changes that signaled Raji's estrus period. This highlights the most difficult part of the management of solitary animals, knowing when to introduce the pair. Females are only receptive and fertile during their estrus periods, which occur in cycles that are governed by hormones released in response to outside stimuli. Depending on the part of the world from which a species comes, the stimulus may be the day's length, or rainfall, or temperature, or some combination of these. The presence of the male may also be a factor. Species from cold climates may have only one estrus, while tropical species may show several. Even in the tropics, most species have distinct birth peaks, when most of the young are born, for birth at the proper time of year, warm enough and with enough food, is important if the babies are to survive.

In the wild, animals can figure out for themselves when a female is receptive by reading signals of scent and sight and sound. A female cheetah begins to call and to spray her scent on rocks (as probably does a female rhino). Attracted by this, one or more males soon arrive to pay court, and often to fight for the right to mate. When captive animals are caged together, they can, of course, answer their own questions about the female's reproductive condition, but when they must be separated, a lone female can be sending signals in many different languages to no avail if no human can interpret these and send in her mate. Although there are some species of animals that show physical changes with estrus, such as the swelling of the genital region so obvious in some species of monkeys, most creatures keep their affairs strictly to themselves.

Changes in behavior, though they may be low key, are often the best indicators of estrus. Keepers know their animals well and note the increased restlessness, the vocalizing—often with new sounds—the placid animal that becomes aggressive or the aggressive one that becomes playful. Animals that are oriented toward humans may display these signs to their keepers, but not all are that obliging, nor is it always really desirable. When a creature is new to the zoo or unfamiliar or an object of special interest, a series of observations help establish a pattern.

Observers record an animal's actions, focusing on certain kinds of behavior for a set period of time every day, anywhere from thirty minutes to around the clock. They use forms broken into time blocks—once a minute is common—where they note every time that a cheetah rubs its cheek or its flanks against an object, when and if it rolls, and whether its calls are purrs, yipes, or yowls. A rhino may honk or whistle and the female pace incessantly at night a few days before mating. Comparing observations from day to day, a behavioral scientist can see a pattern emerge, and if this is repeated monthly, or whatever interval is proper for that species, this pattern could become a guideline for introducing the male. There is no guarantee, of course, that the two will take to each other—the Indian rhinos never repeated their success—for these solitary types can be exceedingly individual, but the stage will be set as far as anyone can arrange it. These osbservations are not used or needed for all species, but they are a great help with the solitary ones.

Considering all the precise scientific tests practiced today, some may wonder why there is not some kind of test, such as the "frog test" used to determine human pregnancy, that can be used to tell when an animal is in estrus. There are such tests, but they are very imprecise for all but a few species. For the tests that are based on changing hormone levels to have meaning, they must be compared to the normal level of that hormone in that species; not only the levels, but the forms in which that species excretes that particular hormone have to be established. This means that there must be a baseline series for each species, something that calls for fairly sophisticated laboratory work, and that takes time.

Nor is obtaining samples the easiest thing in the world. A tiger or a rhino may well resent having blood samples removed, and the procedure, which calls for sedating a large animal, may produce considerable stress, which may in turn affect the results. Handling and sedating a large animal produces a good deal of stress in keepers and vets as well.

If the animal in question lives alone and indoors, urine samples are easier to collect, and this is the usual way that hormone testing is done. If it is a part of a herd outdoors and a number of samples have to be collected, it can be a different story. Lynette Shirley, a keeper at the Dallas Zoo, wrote of her life with the okapis, those plush-furred, mahogany-colored relatives of the giraffe. Trying to establish the estrus cycles of these rare animals entailed daily urine collection from three females. Writes Shirley:

"The fine art of urine collecting is not as simple as the uninitiated might suppose. It entails time, patience, and a warped sense of accomplishment. . . . Having obtained one vial of the precious liquid, the Hill Keeper marches victoriously on to the two remaining females—only to wait tortuous minutes while they munch hay, slurp water, wander around, stare dumbly, and finally—how many days has it been?—Success at last!"

Keepers are the zoo's unsung heroes. Not only do they collect fecal and urine samples and clean cages and devise new entertainments for the apes and watch for signs of sickness or signs of estrus in their charges, but they have to put up with nonsense from those same charges. One must contend with wild asses who wait demurely until her back is turned and then nip her on the rear. Another does her work while a condor tries to eat her shoelaces and a third faces an irate and well-taloned owl every time he opens the cage door, and so on through every line. It is fortunate that most are endowed with a good sense of humor.

Slowly, we are beginning to understand the zoo mating game in all its permutations. To the uninitiated, some of the solutions must seem simple, and one wonders if the animals, especially those of the so-called "impossible" species, have not been wondering why these humans fail to understand their signals. But we have, in essence, been deciphering a strange language without the benefit of a Rosetta stone. Today, we have at least a few key words, the results of which are beginning to show in the birth rates.

A COHORT OF INFANTS

Zoo babies come in assorted shapes and sizes. Kangaroos are born after only thirty days gestation, when the joey, or kangaroo infant, still almost an embryo, makes its incredible journey from the birth canal to the safety of the warm, furry pouch. A baby bear weighs only a few ounces at birth and spends its early weeks in the safety of its mother's den. A baby hippo is born in the water, a little seal on a rocky ledge. Some are born in privacy; some make a public entry into the world, furnishing the zoo visitor with an unexpected moment of drama.

On a sunny April day, visitors line the fence by the Dama gazelle yard, watching with bated breath as a newborn gazelle calf tries to gather its long legs for its first steps. The calf lies at its mother's feet, a damp bundle of incredibly thin legs connected to a delicate head. Its long ears hang limp and dejected. All in all the tiny creature looks as if it needs to be inflated before it can become a proper animal. Its mother, a slender white animal with a russet-brown neck and saddle that glow warm in the sunshine, seems quite undisturbed by her recent ordeal. She stands quietly by, occasionally nosing the baby to encourage it to rise. But those long legs are more than the calf can handle; when it gets its hind legs under it, the front ones collapse; once the front legs are gathered, the hind ones refuse to cooperate. It sinks back to rest. The mother calls—the faintest of bleats—and the baby tries once again. The waiting crowd, some of whom have been there since the birth, is silent, but their encouragement is almost palpable.

Among the visitors, the collection manager stands and watches with growing concern, because these calves are usually on their feet within half an hour of their birth. This one has been trying for almost an hour and the air is growing chilly as the sun moves and leaves the baby in the shade. The manager wonders if she should wait longer or step in and run the risk that the mother would reject her calf? Finally, she calls the vet and within a few minutes his truck pulls up. He eyes the situation with a practiced glance. Because this is an inexperienced mother dealing with her first birth, he decides that all is probably well, and proposes giving her more time to see if she can work it out herself. Sure enough, the calf soon gives a mighty lunge and gains its feet. It wobbles, tries a step, takes a nose dive, and is down again. The waiting crowd sighs.

But the next try is even stronger and more steady. Successful at last, the calf moves to its mother, soon to take its first strengthening meal safe at her side.

Every birth is a drama, but many take place at night or early in the morning, and only occasionally is the public privileged to watch the birth of a gazelle, or the arrival of a giraffe's six-foot infant. These are exciting and often very moving moments, but despite the recent trend advocating natural childbirth for humans, visitors may be upset when they see the process in action. The arrival of baby monkeys in particular brings out a flood of sympathy, and some visitors are concerned to find that the zoo has not furnished a delivery room and obstetrician, as they watch the mother give birth and then clean her wrinkled infant and cuddle it to her. But birth is a natural process, and human help, no matter how well intentioned, can be a source of stress to a wild animal.

Births are major events in zoos. No expectant animal mother is neglected. An animal such as a panda or rhino may have watchers in attendance round the clock as her birth date draws near, sometimes using the closed circuit television that allows a close watch without the intrusion of a human presence. For some, such as bears, even the camera may provide too much disturbance, so only a hidden microphone—or an ear to the wall—helps the keepers to detect the babies' first faint squeals. Often animal mothers are so sensitive that human interference may make them desert the babies or harm them. Soon after their birth, calves and fawns and baby apes have their first physical and get protective immunizations, but many other babies are left strictly alone until they are older.

In their concern, the visitors may not notice the natural support systems that exist among a number of species, including elephants and many of the primates. A monkey mother is often surrounded by other females, animals that may well include the new mother's own mother or sisters, but that, at the very least, are familiar companions. If it is a colobus monkey giving birth to her snow-white baby, which looks like a little white tennis ball in her black arms, there is usually another female close at hand to take charge.

In zoos, new mothers and infants may be isolated from their group or herd or troop for a short time until the youngster is stable, but this isolation does not imply a need for medical care in the hospital but rather, a move to a familiar enclosure near the familiar animals and with familiar keepers. That feeling of security is the best medicine.

The presence of the male may be another story. When the two live together, the first question, and one that has to be settled before the birth, is what to do with father. Not all fathers take kindly to their young. A male bear may be his offspring's worst enemy, which may explain something of the proverbial irritability of mother bears. Male

A colobus monkey looks like a little white goblin at birth, but soon assumes the black and white coat of its parents.

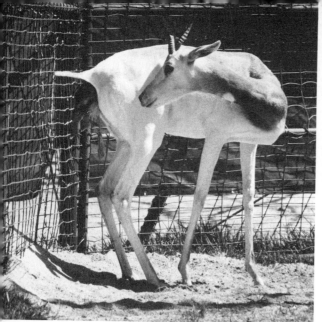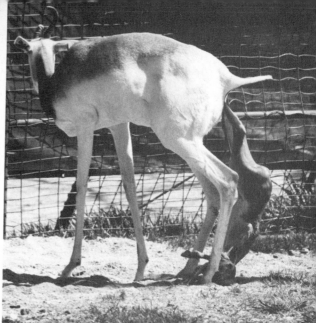

Birth of a Dama gazelle. The calf emerges from the birth canal . . .
. . . and slides, unceremoniously, head first to the ground . . .

monkeys may ignore the baby but pester the mother. And in a great many species, males are really quite unnecessary and the mother does nicely on her own.

Still, there are a number of other species where the male is actively helpful. Fennecs, one of the most enchanting of foxes—tiny, sand colored, with huge ears that seem to have been borrowed from a larger beast—are devoted fathers, bringing food to their mates, guarding the den, and playing with their pups when they emerge. South American bush dogs have been seen gently helping with the delivery of their pups. Both these species only care for the young properly when the male is present.

Even when the father does not seem to play any active role in rearing his young, his presence may add to the female's comfort and sense of security for, in the wild, he would be a protection against predators. So the place of fathers has to be decided early in the game, based on what a curator knows of the species in the wild as well as of this particular individual.

In fact, the whole family may be important to the young. It is not only among tamarins that older siblings or other family members share in the care of youngsters. Dwarf mongooses raise the young in an extended family and young animals may be seen busily feeding babies or carrying them from one place to another in their mouths. It is easy to imagine that these youngsters look a little nervous with this grown-up responsibility, seeming to freeze in horror at what they have done if they drop one of their charges, while a nearby adult moves in to scoop it up and carry it off with fussy efficiency.

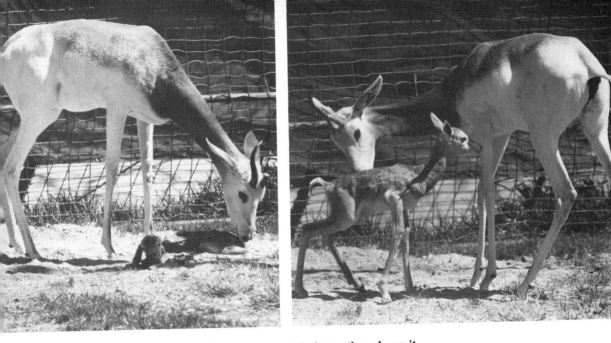

. . . where it lies, weak and limp-eared, while its mother cleans it.
But within half an hour, most calves are on their feet . . .
. . . and finding their first warm, strengthening meal.

When animals lack any of these things that spell safety, they may experience stress, which is not the sole prerogative of overworked businessmen. Stress in animals may result in sickness, reproductive failure, infanticide, and even death. The effects vary from one animal to another, one species to another, and may be more or less severe at different times in an animal's life. Because birth for animal mothers is a sensitive time—a time of strange sensations and new drives—neglected babies or infanticides may be the result of a situation that the animal can not handle. Even well-intentioned help from humans can have unhappy results. Recent studies of animals have provided fascinating and valuable information on those things that affect good parenting.

Tree shrews—long-nosed, squirrel-like creatures from southeast Asia—are among those studied. When tree shrews become parents, a pair must be provided with two nests, one for the babies and one for the parents, for tree shrews have reduced mothering to a minimum. The babies stay in one nest, where the mother visits them once in forty-eight hours to nurse. Then the babies, their stomachs bulging like little balloons, snuggle down to snooze until mother once again returns. Meanwhile, she and the father continue to sleep in their own nest, undisturbed, presumably, by 2 A.M. feedings. There might be something to be said for the system.

Tree shrews react to such sources of stress as overcrowding, sudden noises, and strange keepers by ruffling their tails, so that instead of being furry but slender, the tails look like bottle brushes. If the ruffling is only occasional, the tree shrews are only showing a passing annoyance, but if their tails are ruffled most of the time, there is trouble ahead. As a result of studies, a tail ruffling index, or TRI, has been devised by the German ethologist, D. van Holst, that cues observers to the emotional state of the tree shrews. At even a low level of stress, the tail ruffled less than twenty percent of the time, a mother tree shrew becomes disrupted in her nursing schedule. At any point over twenty percent, she may fail to scent-mark her young, and then eat them. At a TRI of fifty percent she becomes sterile.

Other animals may not have such an obvious and convenient index of stress, but many of the same factors—overcrowding, strangers and strange noises, lack of proper dens—may affect their reproduction. As a result, there are zoo babies that the visitor never sees until they are half grown because these get all the privacy possible.

In 1972, red panda cubs were born to the current pair of those delightful animals at the National Zoo. Red, or lesser, pandas had been exhibited in zoos for years. Changes in their diet and inoculation for canine distemper had improved the survival and health of the adults, but although cubs were born, few survived. Stress to the mother seemed to be the reason for cub mortality.

Immense ears and big eyes make the fennec fox an efficient nocturnal predator, well able to supply his mate and pups with food.

Red pandas look a bit like raccoons, though the relationship is extremely distant if it exists at all, and wholly like some wonderfully cuddly toy. Their Chinese name translates as "Fire-Fox," a name that seems to suit them better than red panda, and speaks of the beauty of their dark red coats. The red of their coats shades into black on their legs, and their white faces have "tear streaks" under their eyes. They spend a good deal of their time in trees and, in the zoo, are most likely to appear as impish faces high in the branches.

Like their very distant cousins, the giant pandas, they feed on bamboo to a great extent, and in their native home in the Himalayas are probably rather solitary. In the zoo they will live contentedly in mixed pairs, but no female will rear her cubs if she has to share her quarters with another member of her own sex.

The 1972 cubs were born in a hollow sycamore tree that stood in their yard, and the first hint that their keeper had of the cubs' arrival was when he saw the mother pacing about with a tiny cub in her mouth. Now anyone who has ever owned a cat with kittens knows that animal mothers move babies quite routinely. In the wild animal it is probably a way to protect the nest from predators, because when the babies are shifted, scents can not build up enough to attract unfriendly attention. But this panda was carrying her cubs in a frantic, nervous way, putting one down only to take it up again and move on. The poor babies were being worn out with the moves and the keepers were afraid that she would carry one up into the tree and drop it.

When unusual behavior of this kind starts, a curator may decide to pull the infant for hand rearing, but red panda cubs had not done well in the past when taken from their mothers, and hand rearing is at best only a one-time solution. Miles Roberts, then assistant curator of mammals, decided to leave the cubs with their mother and, though she already had two dens available, to give her another nest box so that she would have three to choose from. He also cut all human contact to the bare minimum.

At this point, an unseasonable hurricane roared up the East Coast, causing a great deal of flooding and forcing the Zoo to close for three days, an event that gave the red pandas three days of peace from visitors. In spite of the weather, the mother was undisturbed, but when the Zoo reopened, she started her nervous travels again, so Roberts roped off a wide area around her yard and kept the public at a distance. This seemed to be just what the mother needed. She settled down to care for her cubs, and although she moved them several times a day it now seemed a matter of routine. The cubs thrived, and since then the National Zoo has become a leading breeder of these lovely little animals, while other zoos, following the same formula of peace, quiet, and a choice of nests have also had good luck.

A fuzzy red panda cub peers from one of its mother's dens, in this case, a barrel.

There are many reasons why most zoos make great efforts to keep mothers and babies together. One of the most important of these is that the mother's milk is the best possible food for the newborn, supplying not only the right nutrients, but also the required antibodies against disease. Usually it is the most digestible formula for the baby. Sometimes supplemental feedings are provided for a while to help a mother bridge the gap between birth and rearing. Perhaps a young camel will receive a bottle at his mother's side until she recovers from the birth and can take over. One such baby camel was born in the midst of the excitement over the giant panda artificial insemination. But in spite of the distractions, the keepers were able to feed the baby and keep him with his mother. The result was not only a healthy little camel but a delightful exhibit, as the gawky infant gambolled around his mother, nudging her or pulling at her mane, finally snuggling at her side.

Mother rearing is important for most species of animals, but as we have seen, it is especially so for the great apes, and the ideal role model for ape mothering techniques is another ape. Lacking experienced apes as examples, zoo personnel have tried a number of methods designed to show expectant gorillas and chimps what they should do in this situation. The animals have watched films, which they may do with interest, or keepers have given them dolls to hold and instructions on how to hold them, rewarding them with treats when they do it right. In one instance, a human mother demonstrated proper nursing techniques with her own baby before an apparently interested gorilla. Apes are intelligent and imitative and some of these methods seem to help.

Sometimes a keeper can work directly with the mother and her baby. In many zoos, ape keepers spend a good deal of time with their animals, finding ways to add diversity to the lives of these intelligent beasts, and they often build strong and positive relationships with the charges, which can be put to good use when rearing problems arise. A lot depends on the ape when deciding how close such contacts can be, for even a very friendly, well-intentioned ape is a powerful animal, and a misplaced love pat could mean an injured keeper. However if the ape is good tempered and has a good relationship with her keeper, she may, assuming that she has any interest in the baby at all, allow that keeper to touch the baby and position it.

Pat Sass, a keeper at the Lincoln Park Zoo in Chicago, was determined that a chimpanzee that she had helped to hand rear would rear its own baby. The ape was holding the infant, cradling it, but as is often the case, not letting it nurse. It was too high or too low or it pulled at her hair so that she shifted it away from the breast. For five days, Sass worked with her chimp, who had been mildly sedated, scolding her if

Adult red pandas most often appear as impish faces high in the branches of a tree.

Mother-reared herself, Pensi the orangutan has been a good mother to her own youngsters, two generations away from the wild.

Veterinarians examine a new-born orangutan before restoring it to its mother.

she moved the baby, helping the baby to find the nipple and urging the chimp to let him stay there. Gradually, the idea of what nursing was all about penetrated the ape's mind, and she began to help her infant on her own. He was also able to help himself as he grew stronger, and gradually a pattern was established. So this keeper's determination was rewarded and this little chimp was able to grow up in a natural setting.

But even with the best of management, there are times when nothing seems to go right. The mother, ape or other species, may reject her baby, or she may not have enough milk, or it may not be rich enough. Either the baby or the mother may become sick. Occasionally, a baby is delivered by caesarean section and the mother does not

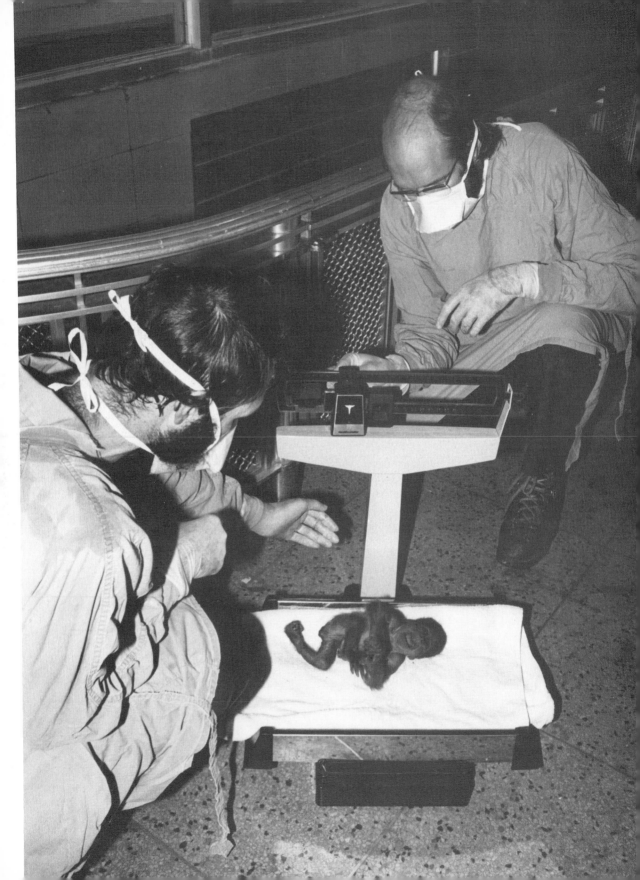

recover fast enough to take on the care of an infant. Even in the wild, females may have trouble with their first born, as if this birth were a trial run, provided for learning. Animals in captivity also need to be allowed to learn by trial and error.

Considering how much of their sexual and parenting behavior the great apes learn from other apes, it is no coincidence that the first second-generation birth of captive orangutans came to a pair of mother-reared animals at the National Zoo. Atjeh (better known to his friends as Junior, and an ape of great charm) and Pensi have produced four babies, and Pensi has been a devoted mother to all of them. The most recent, Tucker, rides on her back like a fur neck piece, when he is not trying his first wobbly steps. Tucker is an object of great interest to young Bonnie, the half-grown female who is the companion and intended mate of Pensi's older son Azy. Watching Bonnie as she watches Pensi care for the baby, seemingly in wide-eyed wonder, reaching out an inquisitive finger when she has the chance, it is clear that something is taking place in her experience that will affect her future.

But Azy and Bonnie are not mother reared. All started well with Azy, with Pensi doing all that could be expected of a mother ape. But one morning, her keepers, Melanie Bond and Walter Tucker, noticed that the baby had an infected lip. Pensi seemed disturbed by this and would pick at it, until the lip became so irritated that the baby had to be taken for treatment. This took longer than expected and by the time the lip was healed, Pensi had stopped producing milk.

Hand rearing was the only choice, and Bond took on the care of the baby. Azy continued to experience crises, a series of infections and reactions to antibiotics that in earlier days would certainly have proved fatal, but after two months of treatment the little orang was healthy once more. Now he needed the company of his own kind, so when the Zoo heard that Bonnie, who was near his age, was also being hand reared at the Rio Grande Zoo in Albuquerque, Dr. Bush, the chief veterinarian, and his wife bundled the little ape in blankets, and with him snuggled on their laps like any infant, flew off to New Mexico. There they left Azy for an extended visit.

With the opening of the National Zoo's new Ape House, Azy and Bonnie returned to join the adults and delighted everyone by adjusting well to family life. Today they are a mischievous pair of adolescents and show signs of interest in each other, an encouraging sign because sometimes animals that have grown up together never show any sexual interest in each other.

The decision whether to hand rear animals must balance a number of factors. Zoos with animal nurseries and children's zoos must fight the temptation to take young animals and place them in these tremendously appealing exhibits. Or sometimes, the

Zoos that have children's zoos and public animal nurseries must fight the temptation to take appealing babies, such as this ruffed lemur, from their mothers for those exhibits.

decision results from too much haste. Many zoo people have a pessimistic streak and tend to expect the worst, pulling a baby, especially one of a rare species, before the mother has proven that she can not care for it. A healthy baby can stand to wait a bit. And many have questions about the wisdom of using hand rearing to try to save an animal that would never have survived in the wild. If such attempts are successful, and assuming that it lives to reproduce, this animal may pass on traits that are against the best interests of the species as a whole. In the wild, first-year mortality runs 50 percent or more for most species; yet in zoos, it is common today to try and save every young animal possible, even though many curators harbor misgivings about the wisdom of their actions.

But there are cases where hand rearing becomes a matter of deliberate policy. Some antelope and gazelles may be hand reared in hopes of making them a little tamer and less likely to panic. It is possible to take the edge off their strong flight response by an early and friendly acquaintance with humans, though the youngsters remain far from tame. A few may be really tamed. At the Conservation and Research Center you may see a deer or an antelope trotting along wearing a halter and lead, as amiable and calm as a goat. These animals are part of the study of the reproductive biology of their species. Thanks to patient taming, they can be handled almost as if they were domestic animals and researchers can milk them or take semen samples without using the immobilizing drugs that affect semen quality and stress the animals.

Hand rearing in zoos used to be a matter of the wife of the zoo's director or some keeper taking a rare and valuable baby tiger or gorilla home to care for. Today most zoos have some sort of nursery, either open to public viewing or offstage, where infants are reared. This care is exacting and labor-intensive and many zoos now use volunteers who work under the direction of the professional staff, caring for anything from a single animal to a small Noah's Ark of creatures. A tiger cub snuggles in a box, a young gazelle occupies a pen, a litter of bandicoots fill the incubator.

Each of these species will probably be getting a different formula in its bottle, or in syringes in the case of a really tiny infant, and be receiving it on a different schedule. Milk is far from being just milk and can vary from that of a seal which contains fifty percent fat and allows the little seal to triple its birth weight in three weeks, to that of a rhino, which has almost no fat at all.

Baby deer and tigers and monkeys have been hand reared in zoos for years and their formulas are usually routine. But even today, there are babies of many other species whose needs are unknown. The marsupials, with their almost embryonic young, are

Dr. Olav Oftedal, the National Zoo's animal nutritionist bottle-feeds a baby tiger whose mother did not have sufficient milk.

Marsupials, such as these red kangaroos, may produce different kinds of milk at different stages in the youngster's development.

among this group. No one knows very much about marsupial milk, which may vary in composition at different stages of the young animal's growth.

Among the marvelous marsupial fauna of Australia and New Guinea are the bandicoots, small animals that look something like rats with very long noses and slender toes. When a litter of bandicoots arrived at Hand-Rearing, still nestled in their dead mother's pouch, the first question that Dr. Olav Oftedal, the Zoo's nutritionist, had to answer was what constituted the right milk for a bandicoot. His formula was successful and, fed with a syringe as they nestled in a substitute pouch in an incubator, the babies grew and thrived and soon were scooting about. So friendly were these young animals that one volunteer was heard to exclaim, "I can't move. There's a bandicoot sitting on my foot!" The story has an only moderately happy ending. The babies grew and were weaned, but then sickness struck and two died. Still, to bring three of them to weaning, and even one bandicoot to adult status, is a hand-rearing first.

Whatever their species, the nursery residents are enchanting little creatures, in spite of their sharp little hoofs and fast growing teeth. As they grow older, the youngsters need exercise and toys, and may have playtimes outside their pens. Like puppies or kittens, they are full of mischief and curiosity. One little red panda learned to climb the counter where food was prepared, like a miniature steeplejack, and unless someone caught her would pull all the menus and memos off the bulletin board. Some babies do become a little spoiled—who can resist playing with a tiger cub—but everyone is very much aware that they must be returned to their own kind as soon as possible and that too much human contact endangers their future adjustment. Soon after weaning, they return to animal life, hopefully as full fledged members of their species, to breed offspring of their own, because even though animals should not be viewed only as breeding stock, successful breeding is a sign that the hand-reared animal has matured with the proper social qualities of its species.

Baby animals form an attachment in their earliest days to their caretaker, normally their mother. This gives them clues about the source of food and warmth and safety, but may also give them an image of their species. This is known as imprinting, a rather

A bright-eyed rat snake is independent from the moment of hatching.

A baby striped owl needs weeks of care and may become attached to its human caretakers.

complex phenomenon that is strongest in early life, but which sometimes carries on into adult years, and which in birds may even affect the choice of a sexual partner. While it is important that animals do not imprint on human caretakers at any time, it is essential if animals are to be returned to the wild. In 1983, four California condor chicks hatched at the San Diego Zoo from eggs taken from wild birds. By 1985 or 1986, some of these may be released to supplement the twenty or so wild condors that still remain in the California mountains. This action has justly received a great deal of publicity, but the prototype of the program was developed at the U.S. Fish and Wildlife's Patuxent, Maryland, Wildlife Research Center and the Bronx Zoo. Since 1966, the Patuxent Center, under the direction of Ray Ericson, has been breeding Andean condors to develop methods that might serve to save their California cousins.

Four pairs of Andean condors now breed at Patuxent, and other zoos have pairs as well. At the Bronx Zoo it was established that by pulling the first egg the great birds would lay a second and a third, as we now know the California birds will do. But pulling eggs means hand rearing, and the question was if hand-reared birds, especially of a species that has a very long dependent period, could be brought up so that they would be able to live free.

In 1980, Donald Bruning of the Bronx Zoo, using eggs from Patuxent and working in cooperation with Stanley Temple of the University of Wisconsin, who would handle the release procedures, started educating chicks for release in South America. This meant that their earliest contacts must be with their own kind.

The chicks lived in a brooder box, where the keepers could watch them through one way glass, but where they could only see each other. They could be lured from one side of the box to the other for cleaning, and when keepers had to weigh them or give them medical attention, they covered the chicks with a black cloth or a hood made from a sock.

Condors feed their chicks by offering them bits of meat in their beaks, so instead of offering their chicks tidbits on forceps in the more usual way, the condor keepers offered food with hand puppets made like condor heads, both male and female models.

An enclosed box may seem a limited environment, but condors nest in deep rock crannies and wild chicks remain in this shelter until they are about four months old, when they begin to go to the edge of the nest and flex their wings. By the time that these chicks were ready for this, they were on their way to Peru; their first view of the outside world was of the mountainous terrain of their ancestors. Wild condors and vultures were lured close by placing baits, so that the youngsters could see the adult birds. Here they lived, still with as little human contact as possible, until they were fledged, when, equipped with solar-powered radio transmitters, they flew off to join the wild birds. Seven of the eleven birds survived and are now living wild.

This gives real encouragement to those who are trying to save the California condor. Such techniques are at best a substitute for the animal's natural way of doing things, but when a species is down to twenty members, such substitutes are something for which to be thankful. It is too soon to say that we can save the condor, but thanks to expert programs of artificial incubation and hand rearing, the future looks far brighter for condors—and for many other species as well—than it has for many years.

FEATHERS AND SCALES

Mammals are not the only residents of a zoo. Salmon-pink flamingos, scarlet and yellow macaws, flotillas of varied waterfowl, giant anacondas, and beautiful and deadly vipers may be among the more popular exhibits, and may also account for the greatest number of individual animals. Until recently, reproduction among birds, reptiles, and amphibians has not been a high priority (except of a few enthusiasts), but the increasing difficulty of replacing most exhibit animals, and the growing number of endangered species, have given breeding a considerable impetus. There are well over four hundred species of endangered birds, from whooping cranes to Hawaiian honey-eaters, and no one really knows how many reptiles and amphibians may be threatened. These are nearly impossible to census, but since they are highly sensitive to environmental disturbances, there are certainly far more endangered forms than the lists indicate.

Although birds and herptiles (a combined term, deriving from herpetology, that saves repeating "reptiles" and "amphibians") follow the same mating systems and are subject to the same influences of their environments that mammals are, they are often more rigid in their requirements. Their behavior is more completely innate and they lack some of the flexibility that some mammals show. In addition, all birds and most herptiles lay eggs, which adds another interesting dimension to their propagation.

About ninety percent of all birds are monogamous, not surprising considering that it takes many weary trips with mouthfuls of food to feed a brood of nestlings, and usually both parents do their share. As a result, it behooves a female bird to be very selective in her choice of mate, considering that his ability as a territory holder and a provider may well determine the success of her whole reproductive effort. Pair formation is one of the greatest problems in raising birds.

Zoo marriages are arranged in the curator's office, often as carefully planned by genealogy as were those of medieval royalty, but where the bride of the Middle Ages had little choice but to go along with the plan, birds have options—and exercise them. They may react to the curator's choice of a mate with anything from a cold shoulder to

The cold yellow eyes of a snowy owl can intimidate both humans and prospective mates.

Male and female black swans look very much alike, but only the female sits on the nest to incubate the eggs.

Standing five feet tall from casqued head to dagger-sharp clawed feet, blue of face and red of wattle, the double-wattled cassowary looks more like a totem pole than a bird.

platonic friendship to attempted murder. Why, of two seemingly similar birds, one will make an instant hit and another be rejected, no one really knows. (In fact, we have been known to ask, What does she see in him?—of members of our own species.)

The first step in establishing a pair is to make sure that the two birds are of opposite sexes, a seemingly simple move that is really not so simple. While experts sometimes err in sexing young mammals (one tigress rejoices in the name of Marvin—the result of a mistake more common in house cats), by the time they reach maturity, it is possible to sex most mammals accurately. This is not true of birds, for contrary to a commonly held opinion, the male and female are colored differently in only about half of bird

species. Male and female adults may show slight differences in plumage or size or eye color, but these often do not appear in young birds and may fall within the normal range of the species in any case. Often an unproductive pair turn out to be two of a kind, while two "females" suddenly startle everyone by laying fertile eggs.

There are several methods of determining sex. Blood or fecal steroid analysis may show differences, or it is possible to use the laparoscope, a slender fiber-optic light source used with a powerful scope. With this a veterinarian can inspect the bird's internal organs through a tiny incision in the abdomen and settle the question once and for all. The procedure does not seem to bother most birds unduly. After such a check, they are soon up and pecking at their food.

Birds themselves may have trouble placing the sex of another bird. All the wonderful varieties of courtship display appear to be designed to clarify this matter, as well as to synchronize and stimulate the nesting cycle. Geese and swans perform a triumph ceremony—bowing their long necks and calling a wild duet—terns present a fish to a prospective mate, herons and cormorants may offer a stick for nest building. They take their cues for further activity from the response to their overtures. If the sexes are alike, the male makes the most of his coloring in his displays and his song serves for further confirmation. Sometimes courtship starts with antagonism, and females will identify themselves by their behavior to deflect male rages, as when a female laughing gull turns her head away from the male so that the threatening black mask of her face no longer confronts him.

A bird may not show much interest in the sex of another bird if they are not in a breeding cycle. The initial problem may be in getting them to simply share an enclosure. Most animals tend to view other members of the same species with suspicion until their status and intentions are proven, for they see their enclosures as their personal territories, and, tending to view newcomers as possible rivals, regardless of sex, act accordingly. If two birds persist in fighting, it may mean that they are really the same sex, but even if they are not, what should be the beginning of a happy relationship may end in a swirl of flying feathers. The introduction of any species has to be made with care, and birds are no exception. Relationships may get off on the wrong foot, so that a female may become the dominant member of a pair, stressing the male into a sort of avian nervous breakdown. One pair of snowy owls reached the point where the male did nothing but huddle in a corner, hardly daring to eat, apparently cowed by his mate's stony, yellow-eyed glare. However, a change in males put her in the proper place for a female snowy owl.

An extreme example of this problem comes from birds that are positively antisocial the greater part of the year but considered monogamous in the breeding season. One such is the cassowary. Cassowaries are one of the largest of all birds, standing about five feet tall from their immense, dagger-clawed feet to the top of their casqued heads. Flightless and unbirdlike in appearance, blue of face and red of wattle, they glare at the observer with the gaze of an evil-tempered totem pole. Their looks are not misleading, for a cassowary can kill with a well-directed kick and are famous for their agressiveness to both humans and their own kind.

In the wild, in Australia and New Guinea, they live alone or in small flocks for most of the year, foraging through the dense brush of the rain forest for the fruits, insects, and small animals that form their diet. Captivity makes them no more social and each bird needs a separate yard—really separate, for they will even try to fight through an open fence—where it spends most of the year in solitary satisfaction.

Even the mating season does not completely overcome their evil tempers. When they begin to show some interest in each other, the male, who is smaller than his mate, is allowed to enter the female's yard for breeding; the meeting is closely watched by a band of wary keepers armed with brooms and rakes, ready to defend him if his intended resents his presence. As the season wears on she begins to accept him, and the two can be left to get on with their courtship; even when she becomes more docile and allows

Breeding must wait upon maturity, a matter of several years in the case of an Andean condor.

To a sarus crane chick, the hanging dowel must suggest its parent's beak. It pecks for food where the dowel points.

makes a sudden move. His gingerly approach and tentative pecks at her back arouse the watcher's sympathy for the poor bird.

Even more amiable birds may be slow to form pairs, and when there is ample room and enough birds a female may be allowed to make her own choice, but Andrew Marvell might have had birds in mind when he wrote, "Had we but world enough, and time,/This coyness, Lady, were no crime." For instance, it took the Bronx Zoo two years and seven birds to establish one breeding pair of Andean condors. Cranes can be very finicky too. If a young female crane is in a run between two males, or if immature cranes are in a mixed flock, they may show preferences, and begin the wonderful calling that forms such an exciting part of crane courtship. When two are placed together, however, things may proceed satisfactorily or they may not. In one such couple, the young female proceeded to turn on her companion after a short time and beat him severely. She was then paired with another male, only to repeat the performance. Returned to her first choice, she apparently changed her mind and settled down peacefully. Maddening though this may be to their keepers, such behavior in cranes and other birds makes sense for their life in the wild since cranes mate for life and usually form pairs a year before they are fully mature. A careful initial choice saves the female from wasting time on an incompetent.

A pair that has settled down together and still does not produce fertile eggs may have to be switched around, or sometimes they can be "egged" on, following the theory that nothing succeeds like success. Since a bird has no way of knowing if her egg is fertile, once she has eggs she will start the incubation process, sitting firmly in place often until long after they should have hatched, even until they explode. Sometimes, it is possible to sneak a fertile egg from another bird into the nest, removing the infertile one. If the new egg is already pipped and about to hatch, she may hear the cheeping of the baby within, apparently a thrilling sound to the birds, who show great excitement. Soon, the chick appears. The birds seem to take this as the most natural thing in the world, and with any luck, the pair will rear the fosterling, and perhaps do better themselves another year. This method has been used with considerable success to reintroduce bald eagles and ospreys into areas where the resident birds still carry a load of pesticide residues, returning healthy birds to the area in the most natural way possible.

Once a pair is found that will at least live together, the bird curator's troubles are still not over. Birds are very sensitive to their environment, to the conditions of light and humidity that govern their breeding in their native lands. Thus, birds that normally nest in the high Arctic may be attuned to the twenty-four hour day of the Arctic summer, and refuse to breed in lower latitudes because they do not have the proper light stimulus.

This response to increased light is not confined to birds of the far north; as I write, it is going on in my own garden. The days are growing longer and the titmice are beginning to call their "Peter, Peter, Peter," though not as intensely as they will in a few weeks. Their songs and courtship displays will start the hormones racing in the females, attracting one to a given male, urging her on toward nest building and readying her for copulation. These activities in turn trigger the formation of other hormones that govern the production of eggs, and the development of the brood patch on her breast. A completed nest and a full clutch of eggs switch off egg production and start incubation. Some internally driven sequence of this kind takes place in all birds, the male to approach, however, it is clear that he is ready to take to his heels if she although they do learn from experience and the process moves more smoothly in an experienced pair.

The amount of daylight that is required to start all this action varies with species and native latitude; in the spring, at the National Zoo, lights burn into the night over the lovely little red-breasted geese, whose home is the Siberian tundra, giving them the impression that they are experiencing the Arctic spring, with its twenty-four hours of daylight.

Group numbers may affect breeding as well as the environment. We usually think of birds as territorial in the sense of the song birds in our gardens, each male claiming his proper patch of tree and lawn and shrub, singing at his boundaries and nesting somewhere within that area. But territories may come in all sizes, from very large to quite small, although probably most birds claim at least a nest territory. Cranes, as a group, need a very large space, and although wild cranes form flocks in the winter, they need complete separation from other cranes when they nest. Whooping and sandhill cranes may need as much as a hundred acres in the wild, though, luckily, they will settle for less in the zoo. This is one reason why such species are so vulnerable to habitat disturbance; they will not breed without a proper territory.

As spring comes on these cranes begin to call and dance, wonderful displays that partake of some of the moves of a square dance—bow to your partner and sashay 'round—at other times more like some of the more exuberant African dances, as the birds leap into the air, sometimes tossing clumps of grass on high. Watching these exuberant displays and listening to the wild, far-carrying voices brings a realization of the loss to the world should cranes no longer cry in the wild. These dances cement the bond between the birds, but it also makes them more aggressive to others of their kind, even other crane species, and adjoining yards have to be separated by covered fences. Even then, male cranes may hang around near the fence, seeming to be on the lookout for rivals.

At the other extreme are birds like flamingos, who will not reproduce until they are part of a colorful, noisy crowd. Breeders have found that unless they have somewhere around sixteen to eighteen flamingos, as a minimum, there will be no breeding. The birds go through highly synchronized courtships, marching together, swinging their heads in unison, seeming to work themselves up to a great coordinated effort. Then they settle down to building cones of mud that serve as nests, usually no farther apart than a bird can peck; just out of reach of a neighbor's long, snaky neck.

And nest sites are obviously a matter of great importance to the birds, who may have very different perceptions of what is proper than the most well informed of curators. No

Territory is an important factor in breeding birds. Sarus cranes require a large yard for each pair of birds.

matter how carefully an enclosure may have been provided with what should be the proper location and materials for a nest, it may lack that certain something from the bird's point of view. At the National Zoo, a satin bowerbird achieved the first North American hatching for her species in a nest built in a recessed light fixture. A cock-of-the-rock built her mud nest in a broom closet, apparently seeing a rock cranny in this space.

One pair of crowned pigeons tried several locations before they were finally satisfied. The largest of the pigeons, these handsome birds are lovely dusty blue with lacy topknots, but they are probably not among the more intelligent birds. In fact, they can act very stupid. This particular pair first tried to build a nest on a broad, varnished wooden railing, although no nest material would stay on the slippery wood. The female sat on the rail cooing and gently flapping her wings while her mate tried to tuck leaves around her, under her, even laying them on her back. As each leaf fluttered to the floor, he doggedly flew down and carried it up again. Finally, the keepers took pity on the birds and built a platform for them on the railing. The pigeons eyed this and promptly departed. Next, they settled on a rock ledge behind an artificial waterfall, and raised several chicks there.

Peace did not last, however for the arrival of a pair of newcomers, satin bowerbirds, upset the balance. A male satin bowerbird does his courting by building a strange structure made of sticks set into the ground that resembles someone's early attempts at basket making. He may decorate this structure with flowers or other objects, blue by preference, and here he displays to the female, trying to lure her into the bower, where they copulate. Just as this male bowerbird got his walls built to his satisfaction, along would come a pigeon and snatch away a stick to put in its nest. The bowerbird in turn plucked sticks that the pigeons had their eyes on. Finally, the pigeons were removed to give the bowerbirds priority. When the pigeons were returned, they again started looking for a nest site and this time selected the branch of a tall palm, which would have offered poor support for a blue jay. Again, the keepers came to their rescue, placing a basket firmly in the tree, and this time the pigeons were willing to accept the help, and have produced one fat chick after another.

Rainfall, or rainfall combined with changes in temperature, is often the trigger for the mating season in tropical species. The rainy season is the forerunner of a good crop of insects for young animals to eat, or provides the right conditions for ducks to nest, or for frogs to lay their eggs, but it is not easy to duplicate. A zoo reptile house is a stable environment, kept nice and warm for the benefit of the inhabitants, but notably lacking in spring showers and monsoon rains. However, a nice warm rain is just what many

Flamingos form pairs, but for breeding also need the stimulus of living as part of a colorful, noisy flock.

herptiles need to start them courting and laying eggs. Even in our own fields the first spring rains bring out the toads, hopping stolidly to the nearest pond, males clasping the females—or the toe of your boot if that is handy—trilling and calling their ancient music.

In a reptile house, the keepers have to find a way to simulate nature if they want to breed frogs. One breeder simply placed his African bullfrogs—animals the size of a saucer that look like green hamburger rolls—in the sink and turned on the tap. The refreshing shower had the frogs eagerly laying eggs within a few days. (More prosaically, but less damply, it is possible to do the same thing with hormone injections, at least with some species.) And when the season is right, a wonderful contrivance of pipes and wires and hoses known as the "frog factory" encourages breeding among a colony of horned frogs.

Amphibians have been the stepchildren of most reptile houses, little noticed by the public, yet they are intriguing and often very beautiful animals. Tiny arrow poison frogs gleam like black-and-green enameled objets d'art. Salamanders wear scarlet or glossy black-and-yellow coats. Tiny tree frogs cling to leaves and walls like so many little plastic magnets on a refrigerator door, their suction-disk toes tucked neatly at their sides.

Although the "typical" tadpole hatches from an egg laid and fertilized in shallow water, and develops there into a frog, the amphibian clan has an amazing variety of rearing methods. There are foam nests on land or water or parents may carry tadpoles to the water in their mouths. Some frogs lay their eggs on leaves and the tadpoles drop into the water when they hatch. Parents carry eggs or tadpoles on their backs, twined around their legs, even in their stomachs!

All of these habits have to be accommodated in captive rearing. The nature of the water itself is important. If it is too acid or too alkaline or too chlorinated, the eggs or tadpoles die. The animals are far from impassive and may be as upset by too much scrubbing and cleaning of their quarters as any mammal. They are often shy and find crowds of visitors disturbing, so breeding colonies are often off exhibit. Fortunately, interest in these creatures is growing and, with this, skill in husbandry.

Snakes and turtles also react to showers and, in season, often become interested in sex after their enclosure has been hosed down. Male snakes may begin to battle for dominance, in maneuvers reminiscent of arm wrestling. Extra humidity may start mating battles among tortoises, sending them like slow-moving armored knights to clash their shells together, each trying to turn his rival over and leave him dejectedly on his back.

A female red-eyed tree frog clings to a wall with her suction toe pads. The smaller male will fertilize her eggs as she lays them.

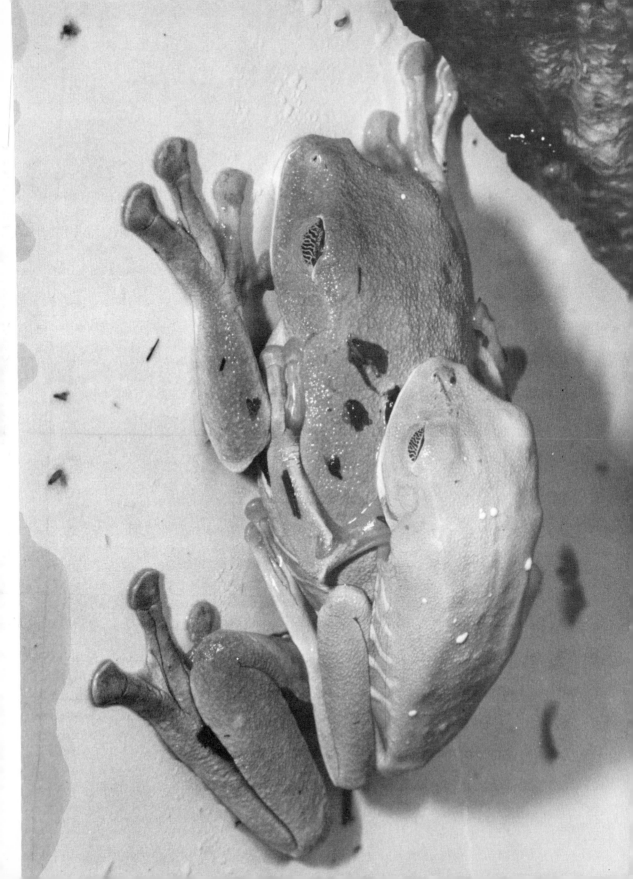

If they are to hatch, a green tree python's eggs need careful control of humidity and temperature.

Sometimes they may overturn a female, either in the process of attracting her attention or by mistake, for some herptiles seem a little vague about the sex of their companions. Frogs and toads will clasp anything that arrives in the matings ponds, but when a male toad is so clasped, he gives a distinctive grunt that identifies himself. Some lizards may judge the sex of another by the behavior of the other animal, the one that responds aggressively to a male's display being clearly another male. Others may use scent as their clue, a male lizard flicking his forked tongue to test another.

Humidity improves scents, which are as important to reptiles as to mammals. A male snake tracks the female, forked tongue aflicker, delicately picking a scent from the air. Females seem to be especially attractive just after they have shed their skins, and if a keeper rubs a moistened shed skin on a female's back, that may bring the male quickly to her side. (As a footnote for snake and turtle fanciers, many of their favorites breed best when the male and female are kept apart.)

For some reptiles, decreasing day length signals the time for winter hibernation. Snakes such as timber rattlers often spend the winter in large aggregations and mate when they emerge in the spring. Because many animals are close together, even though they may be hungry after the long winter, this is the best time to find a mate. The story is told of one early settler in the Blue Ridge Mountains who is supposed to have built a cabin in the fall and awakened one fine morning the following spring to find his home crawling with passionate rattlers whose den was now his basement. Snakes such as these breed in response to the change from cold and dark to warm and light, and some zoos use soft drink coolers or something similar to put them in cold storage for a few months.

For others, the beginning of the rainy season, even in the tropics, means a slightly lower temperature in their surroundings. This may be the signal for the mating season. Changing the temperature in their cage, dropping it at night from 70 to 60 degrees, induced emerald tree boas, surely one of the world's most beautiful snakes, to mate, and in due time, bear baby snakes. The discoveries of factors in the environment that lead to successful reproduction of hitherto "impossible" species proceed by trial and error. This is a process of deciding what variables exist in the animal's natural

A Burmese python incubates her own eggs. She raises her body temperature as much as five degrees by muscular contractions.

Newly metamorphosed oriental fire-bellied toads are the outcome of the careful control of a variety of environmental factors.

environment, then changing each of these methodically and noting the results. Bit by bit, information accumulates, and breeding records improve.

Proper management of these animals leads to mating and, if all goes well, mating leads to eggs. It is hard to say if an egg represents a birth before it hatches, but the care of eggs is the first step in the production of birds and herptiles. An egg is a remarkable life support system, containing all the nutrients that the embryo will need during its development. But without the proper outside conditions, an egg remains an egg. Wild animals have innate knowledge of what has to be done. A wild duck waddles up to her nest, feathers damp as she returns from drinking, pokes the eggs in a haphazard way so that they are partly turned, and flops down to incubate. She knows nothing of temperature or humidity, about the egg's need to breath or give off water, but, at the proper time, most of her eggs will become ducklings.

A turtle digs a vase-shaped hole, deposits a batch of eggs like ping pong balls, scrapes the sand in again, flops and scuffles a bit to compact the sand, and returns to water without another thought for her young. But, unless they are uprooted by predators, little turtles emerge in due time.

In the zoo, it would be ideal if all these creatures could rear their own young, and those birds that have helpless, naked nestlings receive every encouragement to do so.

Success in captive propagation is especially sweet when the hatchlings belong to an endangered species as does this baby Cuban crocodile.

Anyone who has tried to raise a baby bird that has fallen from the nest knows what a demanding and often futile chore that can be. But among birds whose eggs hatch into lively, downy chicks that are able to feed themselves with a little encouragement, artificial incubation is often routine. This is because nests may be disturbed by another passing bird in yards where there are many ducks, and the perfect, predator-proof fence is yet to be invented. While swans and geese may defend their nests well and faithfully against predators, there is always a chance of raccoons or feral cats preying on the nesting ducks; on the average, artificial incubation gives better results.

When the truck from the Zoo makes its run to the Conservation and Research Center, part of its cargo is a large wooden box. Inside, nestled in tiers of plastic foam cut into oval compartments of different sizes, are the eggs that were laid in the preceding week. Bird's eggs do not have to be incubated from the moment of laying; most wild birds lay an egg a day, or every other day, until they have a full clutch, and only then do they settle down to incubate. Disinfected and held at 55 degrees, eggs can await the weekly shipment.

At the Conservation Center, a keeper unpacks the box, making a note of the number penciled on each egg which identifies the egg and its parents. Its history from laying to hatching—or failure to hatch—is part of the records. She then places the eggs in the big incubators where, monitored for temperature and humidity, turned once every twenty-four hours, the eggs rest until they hatch. Duck eggs, goose eggs, crane eggs, emu eggs looking like avocados and cassowary eggs like apple-green grapefruits form the cargo.

The shipment includes a small box that wiggles and emits plaintive peeps. It contains a pochard duckling that hatched at the Zoo and has been sent up for rearing. Before the little duck knows what is happening, the keeper has banded it and placed it in a roomy brooding pen supplied with food and water. She scoops up a mallard duckling about the same age from another pen and places it with the newcomer for company, and to encourage it to peck for food.

Next to the ducklings, a young Inca tern wheezes hopefully at the keeper. She places a small mirror against the side of the pen, for this little bird is becoming imprinted, beginning to think that the keeper is its mother. Seeing its own reflection will help it realize that it is really a tern and make its adjustment easier.

Another advantage to artificial incubation is in the increased annual production of certain species. In the wild, a bird may lose its first clutch to floods or predators, so many species have a fail-safe capability and can lay a second, third, or even later clutch as replacements. Taking advantage of this trait, aviculturalists often pull the early clutches of such birds as cranes and condors, leaving a later one for the parents to hatch. This practice can result in as many as a dozen young birds a season instead of only two.

The care of bird's eggs in zoos has benefitted from the experience of commercial breeders, both of game birds and of chickens; reptiles, however, show more diversity in their requirements. Unlike birds, there are a few helpful reptiles (such as boas) and a few lizards that give birth to living young. Some pythons incubate their own eggs, coiling around a heap of as many as sixty eggs the size of goose eggs and remaining for the entire sixty-day period. These snakes are able to raise their body temperature by as much as five degrees by muscular contractions that make them appear to be suffering from a bad case of the hiccups, thus providing extra warmth that helps the development of the little snakes. Aside from these helpful few, the hatching of reptiles and amphibians in zoos is a fine art that relies on human judgment, for usually the eggs cannot stay in the parent's enclosure. It is hard to keep the proper temperature and humidity there, and they may be disturbed by passing feet, or even eaten.

In an off-exhibit area of the reptile house, such eggs sit on beds of vermiculite or peat, carefully monitored for humidity. Leathery shelled eggs absorb water from their surroundings during incubation, but if they too get much, they may mold; if they have too little, they may dry up. Temperature affects the time that it takes for the embryos to develop, a time which can be many months for some species. This is again a matter of experiment, a trail-and-error process that leads to determining the exact conditions that each species needs for successful hatching.

Artificial incubation techniques do not lead to artificial animals. Rather they are the only possible route to the flock of young emus whose topknots look like the originals of the punk hair-style and who run to the fence to look over a visitor like so many puppies. Or the results may take the form of seven baby Cuban crocodiles, a species nearly extinct in the wild, busily snapping up baby mice under the proud eye of their foster father. Or they may take the form of young peregrine falcons or bald eagles or Galapagos tortoises to be released into the wild. The point is that they work!

THE VET STEPS IN

Everyone concerned with captive propagation would agree that, ideally, all species of animals would live in natural social groups and conduct their mating and raise their babies by the tried and true methods for their species. Within the limits set by space and management, zoo breeding has gone a long way toward accomplishing this. Yet, in spite of everyone's best efforts, there are animals that remain stubbornly uncooperative. A pair may be firmly incompatible, or sexually inept, or socially inept and no amount of behavioral manipulation will change them.

Animals may also suffer from a wide range of physical problems, some the result of captivity, others that occur in the wild as well. Along with behavioral research, the last few years have seen tremendous advances in the veterinary care of exotic animals, which are often quite unlike their domestic cousins, so that now many stubborn behavioral problems can be bypassed by medical means. No one sees this as an all-purpose solution, but it can be a blessing in the short run. The captive populations of many species are still small, so although a curator might wish for a more fertile gorilla or a more cooperative panda, what he has is what there is and he has to make the most of it.

Artificial insemination—A.I. for short—is just coming into its own as a practical technique for exotic animals. It is in common use for domestic animals; around fifty-nine million cows were inseminated by this means in the United States in one year and in some countries ninety-nine percent of all calves start life with the vet as a middleman. After all, why bother with the expense and occasional danger of keeping a bull when semen from a pedigree sire is easily available? Among exotic animals, A.I. has been used most successfully with those that are most like domestic ones, such as the deer and antelope. It's use for the big cats or apes is a recent development made possible by increasing knowledge of hormone levels, improved techniques of handling and storing semen, and improved anesthesia.

A.I. is helpful when members of a pair will have nothing to do with each other, or the male has a low sperm count or is actually sterile. Although this work has been

Rugged play equipment encourages giant pandas to exercise and interact.

increasingly common in zoos, it was the story of the National Zoo's giant pandas, Ling-Ling and Hsing-Hsing, that brought A.I. into the news. This black-and-white pair are the National Zoo's most famous exhibit and possibly its most exasperating inhabitants. From the moment they arrived from China in 1972, two fluffy, playful balls of fur who somersaulted and tumbled about their enclosure, everything was carefully planned so that, in due time, they would become the parents of a baby panda.

Dr. Kleiman, then research zoologist, and the research staff carefully evaluated the somewhat limited information on panda rearing and put this into practice. Captive pandas have in the past become attached to their human companions. The London Zoo's first panda, Chi Chi, flatly refused to have anything to do with the Russian panda An-An, either in London or on a visit to Moscow, although she would display to and court her keepers. To avoid repeating this mistake, Ling and Hsing were firmly treated as pandas, in spite of their beguiling ways.

The Chinese scientists warned that these were solitary animals and that the two should be kept apart except when Ling was in estrus, so they lived in adjoining yards and only contacted each other through the wire of the connecting moon gate. Carefully fed and exercised, climate controlled and meticulously observed, they are probably the most well-studied and -documented animals in the world. But for eleven years, they were total flops as breeders.

We really know very little about wild pandas, for they live in dense bamboo forests on exceedingly rugged mountains that look like the strange, dreamlike ranges shown in Chinese paintings. In this terrain, observation and study are appallingly difficult; observers do well to catch an occasional glimpse of a panda through the thick underbrush. Recently, zoologist George Schaller visited China with an expedition from the New York Zoological Society and the World Wildlife Fund International to assist the Chinese in studying pandas and setting up a panda research center. With the help of radio tracking equipment, he managed to follow a few pandas and learn a bit more about them, but we are still far from knowing them as we do elephants. Even the Chinese, who have bred the greatest number of giant pandas so far, are not successful every time they plan a mating. Although they have fifty or sixty animals in captivity, they only raise one or two litters a year. It almost seems that pandas may be so rare because they have such a complicated sex life.

Probably several factors are involved in Ling-Ling and Hsing-Hsing's unproductive love life; nothing is ever as simple as a single answer. Ling-Ling, the female, is the elder by about a year and, during their first encounters, larger than her mate, so she may have established something of a dominant position. In one of their early meetings,

Interactions are not always friendly. Ling Ling, on the upper level, warns Hsing Hsing away.

she had an injured paw and rolled away from his advances; the next year she was overweight and either could not or would not stand for him. In the wild, Ling, being older in years and like many female mammals maturing earlier, would probably have mated with an older, experienced male, while Hsing would very likely have met an experienced female in his turn. All of this would have helped.

Pandas appear to be very choosy about their partners. The Chinese have found this to be a problem to the point that in one year they had only one male that would breed, and he would only mate with a few favored females. Fortunately, Ling and Hsing do seem to be compatible; they are interested in each other and go through the preliminaries of courtship, though for years there was never a real copulation.

Female pandas are among those animals that have one brief estrus period a year; there are only about three days when it is possible for a baby panda to be conceived. It is essential to know when estrus occurs so that the male can arrive on the scene at the proper moment; it is even more essential to pinpoint the matter more closely and know the time of ovulation for artificial insemination.

Hormone tests are useful for this, but not foolproof. They also take time and, because of this, behavioral observations become extremely important. Dozens of volunteers have spent thousands of hours panda-watching, an occupation that may have its exciting moments when the two potential mates are placed together, or on snowy mornings when they are playful and frisky, but that generally involves many hours of watching pandas eat and sleep. Even in the wild, pandas would spend a lot of time eating because their staple food of bamboo is not terribly nutritious; nor is a panda's digestion very efficient. It takes a lot of bamboo to keep a panda going.

No doubt about it, a lot of behavior-watching is dull; the times when an animal does something really noteworthy are interspersed with many hours when it does very little, but the watcher has to be alert for a change in the normal pattern. The volunteers that undertake behavior watches are not scientists; they are lawyers and housewives and airline hostesses and practically anyone who is reliable and willing to get up in the middle of the night to watch a sleeping panda or a mating rhino. These volunteers are recruited by the Friends of the National Zoo, the Zoo's support society, and receive their initial fifteen hours of training through that organization. Training is an ongoing matter, and they receive much more on the job. Among themselves, volunteers are willing to admit that you have to be a little nuts to do these things—and to do them for love—but it is disconcerting to have public confirmation of this. One watcher, temporarily without a car, called a cab to keep a 4 A.M. shift. When she told the dispatcher that she wanted to go to the zoo, the dispatcher promptly hung up. Grimly

After years of futile attempts, the pandas coordinate their efforts and Hsing Hsing mates with Ling Ling.

the watcher called again, but being wise this time, only gave the street address of the zoo as her destination. In due time the cab arrived, and climbing in, she directed the driver to the Zoo. After a moment of silence, he turned, stared at her thoughtfully, and said, "Ok lady, but you got to pay first."

What do the panda observers see? As Ling-Ling approaches her estrus period, her behavior changes. She loses her otherwise healthy appetite; she begins to pace up and down restlessly and often calls with a sort of bleat. She walks backwards, and she scent-marks often, doing leg cocks to place her scent high on a wall or tree. In the wild panda, these actions would advertise to any males in the vicinity the news that this female was interested in and ready for mating. In the zoo, Ling-Ling's mate, in a separate enclosure, also paces, calls, and scent-marks. If she sees him, she becomes playful and solicits his attention. Once together, Hsing may attempt to mount, but until the 1983 season, he, in scientific terms, "failed to align himself in an effective breeding position."

After several seasons marked by frustration for both pandas and zoologists, Dr. Kleiman and Dr. Mitchell Bush, the chief veterinarian, decided to try A.I. on their reluctant pandas. Their first attempt was in 1980. However, it turned out that Ling had already ovulated and it was too late for her to conceive.

In 1981, the London Zoological Society offered to send their male giant panda, Chia-Chia, to see if a change of mate would prove helpful. It seemed possible that even if the newcomer did not mate with Ling, his presence might stir Hsing to greater and more productive efforts. Chia-Chia arrived in state, accompanied by his keeper, curator, and veterinarian, and was collected from Kennedy Airport and whisked off to quarantine at the National Zoo.

Ling-Ling responded by coming into estrus ahead of schedule, forcing an introduction of the two animals much earlier than had been planned. There is a theory around the Zoo that if Ling can find any way to make life more complicated for her keepers, she will do it. In any case, the two pandas were released into Ling's yard one rainy evening. But instead of courtship, there was battle. Chia-Chia did not take to Ling-Ling at all; instead, he attacked her savagely. By the time the two were separated, he had bitten her several times. For all their cuddly looks, giant pandas have teeth like bear traps, great crushing mills that are designed to chew tough bamboo and are highly effective weapons for biting. Obviously, Chia-Chia was to be no help; not only did he not care for Ling, she was so severely injured and shaken by the attack that there could be no attempt to introduce Hsing who, stimulated by the scent of the stranger, had been creating quite a rumpus in his own quarters. So ended the 1981 season.

Ling Ling stands and reaches for a carrot, enabling panda watchers to check her for signs of pregnancy.

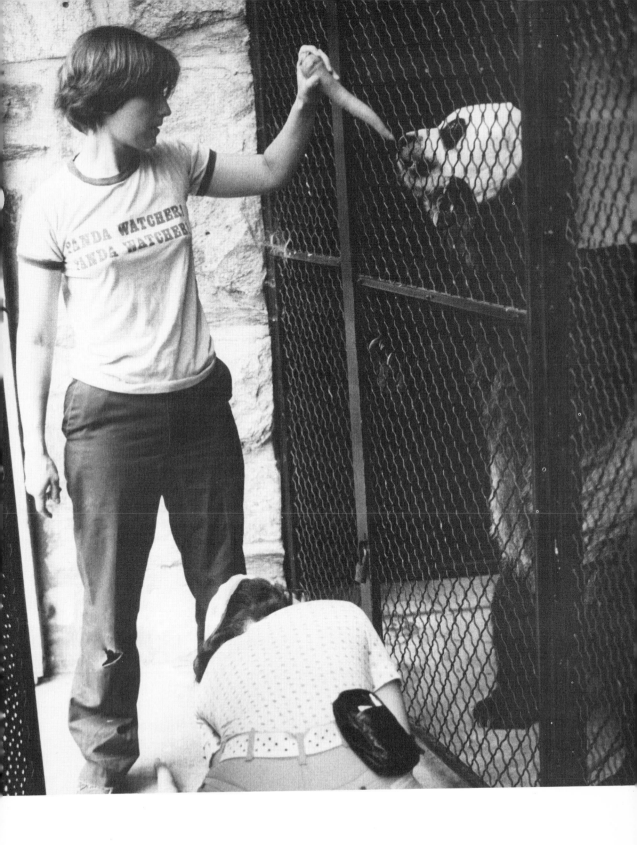

In 1982, everyone was determined to have a baby panda. All through the preceding winter, the two animals had spent more time together, in the hopes that they would be more at ease with each other when mating time rolled around. No one could claim that the pandas were enthusiastic about the new arrangement, but they got along well enough. Ling was carefully watched for signs of estrus, and when the time was right the two were again introduced, with the usual outcome: lots of preliminary action but no results.

Now things moved rapidly, for a panda's estrus only lasts for three days. The plan for A.I. was ready to be implemented. Three zoos were involved, motivated by a common concern for the future of pandas. Urinalysis to determine hormone levels was done at the Bronx Zoo; semen was donated by Chia-Chia in London; Ling-Ling belonged to the National Zoo. On a March afternoon, Dr. Bush and his staff anesthetized Ling and inseminated her with Chia-Chia's semen, which seemed to be of better quality than Hsing's. He also laparoscoped her to inspect her ovaries, finding that she was just about to ovulate. The next day, there was a second A.I., using semen from Hsing, followed by a third insemination the following day. A second laparoscopy showed that she had just ovulated. Medically, the procedure could not have gone better, the timing seemed ideal, and aside from showing a certain lingering dislike for veterinarians, Ling was none the worse. Everyone sat back with crossed fingers to wait.

This was in mid-March. By June, urinalysis by both the Bronx and the London zoos showed no change in hormone levels, but later tests did. Pandas are so stocky and furry, and their cubs so tiny—four ounces at birth—that their looks change very little during pregnancy. Only when birth is near do they show changes in behavior and a swelling of the nipples. As a result, anxious keepers spent much time luring Ling to stand, holding carrots or apples on high, so that they could get a look at the state of her nipples.

At the end of July the Panda House was closed to give the hopefully expectant mother as much privacy as possible, and volunteers started a twenty-four-hour watch over closed-circuit television from the kitchen next door, where they were surrounded by a battery of cameras and tape recorders. This equipment offered another volunteer a moment of glory—of a sort. On a night watch, one of Washington's torrential summer rains sent water flooding into the kitchen where he sat. Frantically the volunteer splashed about the flooded floor, moving all the recorders and cameras to high ground. Finally, all secure, he retired to the adjacent bathroom. As he opened the door, the flood waters poured in after him, vanishing with a swoosh and a gurgle down the floor drain. The next morning a neat notice told others, "In case of flood, go to the bathroom."

Panda-watching continued. A TV monitor was even installed in a nearby building to give the public a view of the animal that many of them had traveled long distances to see. Although some found it frustrating to have only a shadow panda to watch, most caught the excitement over the potential cub and watched the screen with interest.

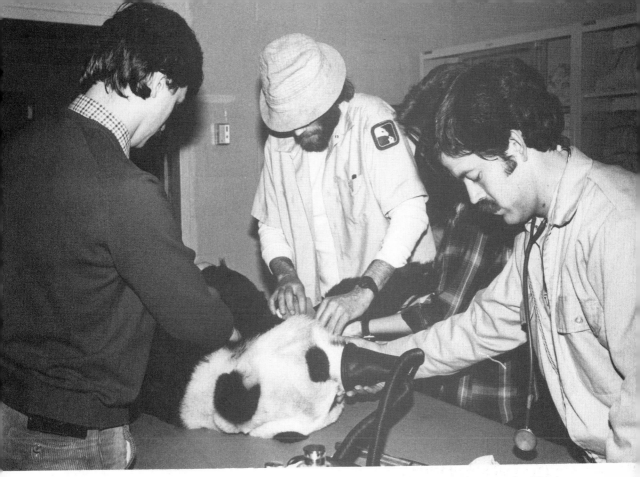

John Knight of the London Zoological Society and Dr. Michael Bush prepare for Ling Ling's artificial insemination. Donald Jensen, National Zoo veterinary resident, administers the anesthetic.

At this point, Ling began to carry nest material, piling bamboo in a corner, but then sitting down and eating it. She began to lick her genital area spasmodically, and, for a time, lost her appetite. But then her appetite returned (one volunteer watcher remarked that "she really pigged out"), the hormone levels fell back to normal, and the excitement quieted again.

The watch continued as long as there was any hope. It is hard to calculate a panda's gestation period. They are thought to have delayed implantation, i.e., the fertilized egg begins to develop but then goes into a resting stage before it implants in the uterus. The average gestation seems to be about 144 days, but there is at least one Chinese record of 175 days. On August 27, Dr. Reed announced the end of the panda watch, with no baby panda but with a tremendous amount of panda information. Volunteer observers had logged 1,365 hours of observations in addition to those of the professional staff.

Even after the watch had ended, Ling would take an apple or carrot and nurse it as if it were a cub. Something clearly had happened, and Dr. Kleiman now thinks that Ling had a pseudo-pregnancy, something in her brain misinterpreting the signals from her body and telling her system she was pregnant when this was not so. Pseudo-pregnancies are not rare in the animal kingdom, although no one is sure why they happen.

Despite the National Zoo's disappointment, A.I. does work with pandas. While Ling was having her pseudo-pregnancy the giant panda at the Madrid Zoo gave birth to twin cubs conceived through A.I., with Chia-Chia as the semen donor. One cub died, but the other is thriving. The Chinese have had some success in this area as well.

At the National Zoo 1983 started to shape up as another discouraging year for the panda breeders. Philosophically the Zoo prepared for another A.I. Simply as a matter of routine, Dr. Kleiman released the two animals in a clammy, March rain for a last encounter. Bleating eagerly, Hsing began to pursue Ling, and back and forth through the yard they padded, shaking the rain from their fur, dashing through their pond as if it wasn't there. Ling occasionally delivered a snarl and a swat to Hsing, but he continued his pursuit. As Dr. Kleiman watched their performance without enthusiasm, she suddenly heard Ling give a vocalization she had never heard before from the panda. She could hardly believe her eyes, for Ling was standing for her mate, and Hsing had finally achieved his goal. Now there was truly cause for hope; to play it safe, Ling was inseminated the following night with semen from Chia-Chia.

Again the watch began, and in mid-July Ling began nest building in earnest. She piled bamboo in a corner of her enclosure and settled in for a restless, uneasy evening, moaning occasionally and showing discomfort. Bess Frank, the collection manager, and Barbara Bingham, the keeper leader, returned to join the Friends of the National Zoo volunteers in watching and waiting, and at 3:18 A.M. the long awaited cub shot into the world to lie on the floor beside its mother.

Both lay still, and the watchers held their breaths. Ling suddenly moved and touched the cub, and as she did it started to cry, emitting an incredible volume of sound for such a tiny animal. Covered with sparse, white hair, blind, and poorly developed, it had a surprisingly long tail, tiny claws on its paws, and a sizeable mouth. Ling turned to her infant and enveloped it in her great mouth, where it almost disappeared. The watchers held their breaths as gently she cleaned the cub, cradled it in her paw in proper panda fashion, and in general acted like a model mother.

At first the cub moved vigorously and hopes were high, but by 6:30 it had stopped moving and despondant watchers realized that it was probably dead. For another ten hours, until Dr. Bush was able to distract her, Ling continued to cradle her dead infant. An autopsy showed that it died of an infection that it had contracted while still in the uterus.

Disheartening and depressing though the loss of the cub was for everyone, at least it

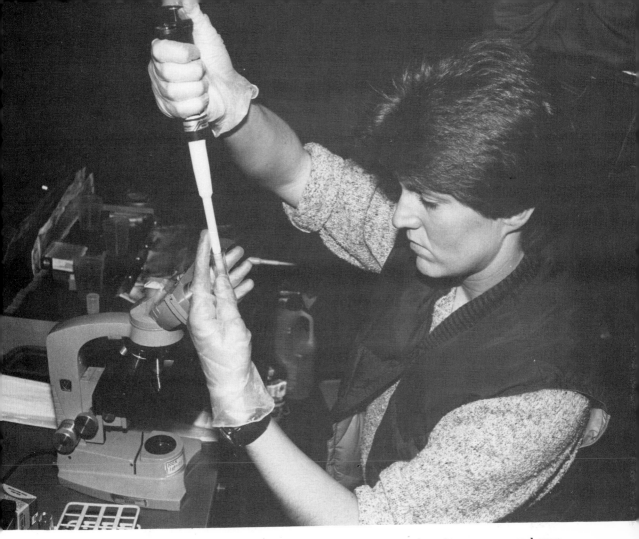

Dr. Jo Gayle Howard examines a semen sample. Frozen preservation of semen, ova, and even embryos is adding a new dimension to captive propagation.

established that Ling could bear a cub, that she would be a good mother, and later tissue studies established that Hsing was indeed the father. Hsing seems to have taken his success to heart, for 1984 saw at least two enthusiastic matings. These were fruitful, but ended in another heartbreak. The cub was born dead.

All of this effort may seem like a tremendous fuss to produce one baby animal. The point is that pandas are unique animals. They belong to a monotypic genus—one that is the sole member of its taxonomic family—that is rare even in its native habitat. And because that habitat is shrinking, the species is under pressures there that make its survival uncertain, even with strict protection. Pandas seem to have a complicated mating system, and the intense efforts to unravel the mysteries would seem essential to make their survival as a captive population much more likely. The fate of pandas represents a scientific conundrum of some magnitude, a major challenge to the experts in captive propagation to prove the technique's worth. In addition, pandas are one of those species like the whooping crane or the California condor that have become symbols of the fight to preserve all endangered species. The importance of saving a symbol may be greater than that species' actual place in the scheme of things, for if we fail there, the doubters can say, "Aha, we knew this wouldn't work." For this reason, if for no other—and there are others—pandas are important.

A.I. has a great potential for increasing the populations of rare animals that have low numbers in captivity. Still, it is a new technique for exotic animals and no one should expect success every time. Out of eighty-three attempts to conceive chimpanzees by A.I. only four have been successful, but we should remember that even in humans, only about one attempt out of four takes. It is essential to know the exact time of ovulation, for the female must be at precisely the right stage of her cycle. The semen must be handled properly and stored carefully. If it is frozen, the proper method of treatment and storage has to be determined, because different species are unlike in this, as in much else.

Research in A.I., semen storage, the storage of ova, and other techniques of artificial reproduction and long-term preservation of genetic material is another part of the Species Survival Plans. Zoos are in an excellent position for this work; in fact, no one else really has the animals and experience. Somewhere, far down the line still, but very much more than a dream of science fiction, lies the day when semen will be routinely transported instead of animals. This is quicker and safer, for although most animals travel well, there is always a little risk involved in the sedation and handling that is needed. A new animal has to be acclimated to a new setting and settled into a new group, and by the use of A.I., all of this can be bypassed.

Ultimately, it may be possible to obtain semen from animals in the wild and bring it into the zoo to increase genetic diversity without taking creatures from the wild; and it will be possible to inseminate wild animals with semen from the captive population. As the technology progresses, it will also be possible to store semen and ova for use in the future, preserving rare gene combinations from an individual living today to enrich its species tomorrow. The so-called "Frozen Zoo" is a thing of the future, but not the too-distant future.

Any process, however, remains vulnerable to human error. In 1982, Dr. E. Michael Douglass and his staff made plans to inseminate a female gorilla at the Memphis Zoo, using semen from a male the Yerkes Primate Center in Atlanta. At the proper time, Yerkes sent off two semen samples, one fresh for immediate use, one frozen as a back up. The staff in Memphis were ready to go as soon as the semen arrived, but the scheduled flight came in without it. In spite of the special handling instructions, the airline had lost the shipment! After several, probably highly irritable hours on the

Even in the zoo world, there is always an ad man. Most animals travel in plain serviceable crates, but the occasional animal celebrity is treated accordingly.

phone, Dr. Douglass located the lost semen, still sitting in the Atlanta airport, where it had been moved to an area reserved for dangerous cargo because it contained dry ice! By the time the semen finally reached Memphis, the fresh sample was useless, but the frozen one was still marginally useful. Dr. Douglass went ahead with the A.I. procedure, and 235 days later a live baby gorilla was born, the first conceived by this technique. In captive breeding, there are more things than animal quirks to contend with; there are human foibles as well.

Such human errors do occur, and probably always will, but it is easy to exaggerate their importance. The fact is that new techniques hold great promise. There are other procedures now being developed that may help bypass other roadblocks in captive propagation. Hormone treatments of various kinds are becoming more common. Not only can frogs be induced to breed without artificial monsoon rains, but such mammals as gorillas, which are often plagued by low fertility or actual sterility may benefit from treatments that have been successful in human males. This, combined with better housing and social stimulus, may help increase the captive gorilla population to safe levels.

The technique of super-ovulation and embryo transfer, borrowed from the livestock industry, where it is used to allow a high quality cow to produce several calves a year, promises rapid expansion of a small population. At the Bronx Zoo, there was a gaur calf, now a bull, that called a Holstein cow its mother. The gaur is a wild cow from India, a big, handsome animal with a red to dark-brown coat and white stockings. They are very rare today in their native land, where they have to compete with domestic cattle for fodder and are exposed to the diseases of their competitors. They are also rare in captivity.

In 1980, General Curator James Doherty and Veterinary Resident Janet Stover, who had been speculating on this technique, decided to try embryo transplant with the gaur. With the advice and assistance of Dr. James Evans of the University of Pennsylvania, they selected several Holstein cows to serve as foster mothers. These cows then had a series of hormone injections that brought their reproductive cycles into the same phase as the gaur cow. The gaur received an injection that made her produce a number of ova instead of the usual one or two. She then was bred by the gaur bull.

A few days later, Dr. Evans washed the fertilized eggs, about the size of a period (.), from the gaur's uterus, placed them in a flask, and carried them off to the laboratory. Since zoo vets like to take full advantage of any occasion when an animal is immobilized, Dr. Emil Dolensek, the chief of animal health, gave the gaur a physical exam and trimmed her overgrown hoofs. A few months later, she was bred again and bore her own calf.

Dr. Evans transferred the ova to the uteri of the four waiting Holsteins, and all sat back to wait for results. One cow came into estrus after a month, showing that the ovum had failed to implant. One aborted after six months for an undetermined reason. At nine months, the third gave birth to a stillborn gaur calf. All hopes now centered on Flossie, the remaining Holstein. Dr. Stover and Dr. Evans could tell that the calf was alive, but it was also past due. Finally, they gave the cow an injection to induce labor, and forty-eight hours later, she gave birth to a healthy, 73-pound male gaur. Flossie has had the privilege of raising her calf, something that she would have been unlikely to do in her normal dairy life, but she must have felt at times like the hen that hatched a brood of ducklings, for the little gaur, in spite of his placid foster mother, showed all the wildness of his natural parents.

For a first attempt at a new technique, twenty-five percent is a good score. Embryo transfer will probably be used most for species that are similar to domestic cattle and that have a close relative ready for fostering. The Bronx-Zoo is now thinking of using the technique to propagate the Arabian oryx, using the gemsbok as a foster mother. Already, a horse has fostered a zebra foal.

By combining A.I. with embryo transfer, we might be able to perpetuate the genes of a very rare animal that is incapable of breeding normally. Part of an ambitious project at the Dallas Zoo, in cooperation with the Brookfield, Oklahoma, and San Diego zoos, involves Lynette Shirley's work of urine collection. This procedure is needed to determine the hormone levels among the okapis in an attempt to expand the okapi population by artificially inseminating an animal that cannot breed normally, and then foster her ova in another animal.

Such techniques, now in their infancy, may well offer the best hope for the long-term preservation of wild animals. Many authorities feel this to be the case. It may sound like the wildest kind of science fiction, but it is theoretically possible to preserve frozen, fertilized ova from animals living today and foster these in animals living many years from now. In this way, we could preserve those rare gene combinations and be sure of having fresh strains to introduce in later years when captive populations, and wild ones as well, may stand in dire need of such reinforcement. It sounds artificial and it is. But by our actions, we have forced our wild animals into highly artificial situations and, at the present time, there seems little hope to look for any change. The least that we can do is to use the technology that we vaunt so highly in their behalf.

THE FINITE ARK

The following item appeared in a recent issue of AAZPA's monthly newsletter: "Golden lion tamarins (*Leontopithecus rosalia rosalia*) are now available on loan for exhibit purposes as single sexed groups or sterilized pairs. These are animals that are surplus to the needs of the International Breeding Program and are now housed at a variety of zoos. Institutions receiving exhibit animals will be required to sign the Golden Lion Tamarin Research and Management Agreement and adhere to the recommendations of the Management Committee."

Here, after all the criticism of single sex groups (other than bachelor herds) and postage-stamp collections, after emphasizing the importance of each animal in the captive population doing its part, are the managers of these endangered animals encouraging their use for non-breeding exhibits. What is this all about?

This question has two answers. First, as the captive population grows, there may come to be more animals than are needed for breeding, and there will be some animals that should not be bred. This is less likely to happen in the growth phase of the captive population, when every animal counts—no one would try to control the size of the okapi population, for example; okapis are hard enough to breed—but it may occur when the numbers needed for a stable population are reached. Animals grow older and pass their peak reproductive years. Although many males in polygynous species can be used in exchanges, probably not all would be needed. Managers would try to avoid using as parents animals that are descended from founders whose genes are over-represented in the population, nor would they choose those that carry hereditary defects if there were an alternative. Ironically, a successful program results in some animals that have no purpose within the program, and the more successful the program is the sooner that is likely to happen.

The second answer is that the zoo ark is distinctly finite in its capacity. If the world's zoos were laid end to end, or side by side, they would cover only about 20,000 acres, or according to William Conway, Director of the Bronx Zoo, would fit neatly into the Borough of Brooklyn.

Of that space, many acres are devoted to roads and lawns, storage buildings and workships, parking lots and concessions—in short, people space. This limits the

Destruction of its habitat endangers the jaguar today and makes its reintroduction unlikely in the foreseeable future.

animal space. It is impossible to cram many more animals into existing enclosures, for this results in increased stress to the animals, increased danger of disease, and the disruption of behavior patterns. Overcrowding may even stop breeding in many species. Zoos are already trying to cope by reducing the number of species they exhibit, providing room for more members of existing species. Space for bachelor herds is in short supply, space for large species like white rhinos diminishing, and this will continue to be a problem. The present capacity of the world's zoos will determine the number of species that can board the zoo ark.

The more successful captive propagation programs are, the more pressing the need for space will become, and zoo directors, zoo support societies, the AAZPA, and almost every organization engaged in captive propagation are looking for solutions to this problem. More of such extensive outlying facilities as the National Zoo's Conservation and Research Center, the Bronx Zoo's Wildlife Survival Center at St. Catherine's Island, Georgia, and the San Diego Zoo's Wildlife Park would help. The AAZPA is talking of arrangments with certain of the owners of western ranches who maintain herds of exotic animals for hunters, but who also feel a strong interest in conservation, to locate herds of rhinos or zebras in protected corners of their land.

There will be an expansion of such facilities, but space is not the only finite thing in the zoo world. Budgets are as well. Land itself is expensive and is only one item to be considered in setting up such establishments. These require miles of high fencing, water supplies, buildings (even if these need not always be elaborate), and other amenities. They require keepers and medical facilities and the availability of veterinary care. There is no zoo director who does not envy Noah the mandate he received: "Of fowl after their kind, and cattle after their kind, of every creeping thing on the earth after his kind, two of every sort shall come unto thee to keep them alive," but Noah was blessed with an ark of infinite capacity and no budgetary concerns. Modern Noahs must find ways to enlarge the zoo ark, and to stabilize the number of passengers that it carries.

One option available to them is to practice birth control, to breed animals on a schedule that will allow supply to balance demand. It is not only zoo demand for exhibit animals that determines this, but the need to schedule the birth of young animals during the adults' peak reproductive years and time their arrivals in such a way that a population remains in balance, plenty of young vigorous animals coming along to replace their elders.

Such a schedule can be set up for each species by building mathematical models of what will happen to the age structure of, say, the lion population, in ten or twenty years if a lioness has a litter of X number of cubs every year, or every other year, or every five years, and plan breeding accordingly. It is then a matter of deciding on the best method of birth control.

Orange male meets white female tiger in a match that was planned according to the genetic background and future placement of the prospective cubs.

One method is contraception. For lions and tigers and others of the big cats, it is possible to implant a capsule under the female's skins that will slowly release hormones and effectively prevent conception for up to two years. These are easy to remove before the time is up if it seems that particular cat should be bred, but in the meantime she can live a normal social life. Contraceptives are used in safari parks for lions that might otherwise be too prolific, and they allow jaguars to live together without fear of unwanted cubs. It is ironic that, in spite of being an endangered species, jaguars breed so well in captivity that there is already a surplus in zoos, and a surfeit of even such a wonderful animal as a jaguar presents insurmountable difficulties.

Although contraception seems to be simple and effective and altogether the ideal method, there are not yet suitable contraceptives for all species. Although research is proceeding to develop others, at this time birth control often means keeping animals as singles, or in single sex groups, or resorting to surgical sterilization. Sterilization removes all possibility that the animal can ever be bred, but even separation may mean

that some animals lose interest in sex, or even the capacity to breed. We have already talked of the complex hormonal feedbacks that affect breeding, and these may be turned off permanently without a stimulus. Exotic animals are not just machines, programmed to produce a baby at the push of a button. Many must be allowed to do things their own way.

Today we hear a lot about biological time clocks, the need to have children during the peak childbearing years. The same is true for animals. Although most seem to retain the ability to reproduce for a greater part of their life span than humans do—it is not unusual for a supposedly post-reproductive female to produce an unexpected infant—there is still a best time for this. This varies with the species, how long it lives, how often it would bear young under natural conditions, and other factors. Any plan has to take into account that species' own method of family planning, another of those strategies by which a species meets the challenges of life in the wild.

In the wild, a large animal such as a tigress might have her first litter of cubs when she is four or five years old, and then expect to average one litter every year-and-a-half to two years—assuming some of the litter survived—for another six or seven years (assuming she lived to be eleven or twelve years old; some might live longer). Which would mean that, in the wild, she could expect to bear three or four litters in her lifetime. Though she could probably produce more than that in the zoo, it would be no particular hardship to restrict her to two litters during her peak years.

However, other species have less leisurely approaches to producing offspring. In Madagascar, there live some ten genera of tenrecs, little insect eaters that—according to Dr. John Eisenberg and Dr. Edwin Gould, Curator of Mammals at the National Zoo, who studied them in their homeland—are probably the closest thing we have alive today to the first mammals to appear on earth. Like much of Madagascar's unique fauna, several of the tenrec species are endangered.

The striped tenrec is a comical-looking creature well covered with spines, resembling a perambulating cactus. Among the quills on its back, there is a patch that rub together as the animal moves around, producing a high frequency sound. This seems be the way in which the mother tenrec keeps in touch with her large litter of babies while they are foraging, just as a mother duck keeps up a low level conversation with her brood.

A striped tenrec can produce ten or more young at a clip, but she can expect to live only about two years, even if she is very lucky. And, because of seasonal changes, she is likely to produce young only once or twice during that short lifetime. Probably most

Rothschild's mynahs, with a substantial captive population, may soon be reintroduced to their native Bali.

never have more than one litter, for few small animals—in fact, few animals—live out their full life spans under natural conditions.

A colony of these striped tenrecs at the National Zoo bred very well, even producing a third generation; in fact, they did so well that they outran the available space. The males and females had to be separated until more space could be found, and this seemed to be a safe enough procedure. Although no one was sure how long their reproductive life might be, for this could not be established in the field study, it seemed safe to assume that it would be similar to that of some other tenrec species, a matter of several years. It turned out that striped tenrecs are different; they reach reproductive senility at the age of eighteen months. When pairs were once more put together, most of the animals had reached this point, and the colony died out. Here is an example— and although an extreme one, there are other similar species—of a species with which one cannot practice birth control, or even delay reproduction, but which must breed steadily if it is to survive in captivity.

So although population growth can be limited to some degree, increases will occur, and there are going to be extra animals. Where are they to go? In the wild such populations remain generally stable over time, and in a rough balance with their habitat, due to natural attrition. Depending on the species, probably less than fifty per cent of the youngsters born in a year live to see their first birthdays; often it is many fewer than that. Of ten young song sparrows, probably only one lives to breed in its turn. George Schaller estimated that about sixty-seven per cent of the lion cubs born during his study in the Serengeti Park died during their first two years. They starved, or were abandoned, or were killed by other lions or hyenas, or drowned, or were victims of disease. And even adults must face many hazards of disease, parasites, and predators. This is a fact of animal life.

All of those responsible for managing wild animals, whether in zoos or reserves, face a similar fact. If small populations are to be healthy and stable over a long period, it will only be by careful observance of genetic and demographic principles. Probably these will never be implemented to perfection, but SSPs are based on managing animals along these lines. Eventually, this will mean removing animals from the breeding population. To meet this need, a number of options are available depending on the circumstances, among these being euthanasia.

The public seems to accept calmly, or perhaps prefers to turn a blind eye on, the euthanasia of millions of perfectly healthy dogs and cats every year by humane societies. And many have had the personal experience of facing the decision to offer a well-loved pet a last act of mercy. Nevertheless, euthanasia in the zoo can arouse public emotions to the boiling point.

In 1982, Steve Graham, Director of the Detroit Zoo, called together the senior veterinarian, the curator of mammals, the tigers' keeper, and other staff members to consider the future of four Siberian tigers. Three were elderly animals that were in very poor health. They were suffering from kidney problems, had bad teeth and gum disease, and one had a hip dysplasia that made movement acutely painful. The fourth tiger was fit and healthy, but so aggressive that she was extremely dangerous to other animals and, therefore, could never be bred. Tigers have been known to kill other tigers, even during mating.

Graham and his colleagues discussed the alternatives and finally agreed that the four tigers should be euthanized. A day or so later, a curator who had not been at the meeting suggested that the aggressive young tiger could be used in a study of artificial insemination, and she was granted a reprieve.

To put this firmly in perspective, three of the tigers were at that point that our dog or cat may have reached on that day when the vet says, "I can give you a geriatric food, but he won't like it. I can give you a medication for the kidneys, but it will only help temporarily. It hurts him to walk and will get steadily worse. It is up to you to decide what to do." The fourth tiger was equivalent to the dog that has chewed up every other dog in the neighborhood and killed the cat next door.

News of the Detroit decision aroused a wave of popular opposition. Graham had earlier made a statement about the overcrowded conditions in some zoos and its serious effects on the animals' well-being, and had raised the possibility that, in time, euthanasia might be necessary to meet this. Although the first news stories did mention that the tigers were ailing, the writers also referred back to these earlier remarks. Angry letters and phone calls poured in from all over the country. These were answered by zoo staff, explaining the true condition of the tigers, and many individuals softened their tone, some even writing again to apologize for their misunderstanding and misplaced anger.

In the midst of this, a Detroit citizen filed a suit against the zoo, accusing the Director of acting in "an arbitrary, capricious, and malicious manner." The court issued an injunction to delay the euthanasia of all four tigers, in spite of the fact that the fourth, the aggressive one, was no longer at any risk.

In the following weeks, public sentiment shifted to support the zoo's position, and the press became firmly supportive. The zoo's medical advisory council, made up of medical doctors, dentists, veterinarians, and biologists reviewed the case and fully supported the zoo's decision. When the case came to trial, the judge ruled that the zoo had not acted in an "arbitrary, capricious, or malicious manner," but that the decision had been reached by "professionals acting through a 'reasonable' process." The court also ruled that the actual condition of the tigers was not at issue, but then continued the injunction against disposal of the aggressive tiger. This was by then an academic point, but left the issue unresolved.

It is not an academic issue however. The three Detroit tigers were in such poor physical condition that their death was indeed a merciful act. It was also an act that made room for young healthy tigers, by the means that nature would use—the removal of the defective and incurably ill. But the time may come when younger animals may have to be removed from the breeding population. At about the same time as the Detroit case, the Copenhagen Zoo in Denmark announced the euthanasia of two perfectly healthy young tigers because there was absolutely no room in that zoo, or in any other, for them.

For any of us who have had to order the death of a well-loved pet, the Detroit decision should be understandable. This is the last act of kindness that we can offer to a suffering animal in our care. The Copenhagen decision is admittedly much harder to deal with. We may see the need intellectually, but for all of us who care for animals, euthanasia produces a strong emotional reaction. Even the word carries connotations that such euphemisms as "culling" do little to defuse. It is extremely important to realize that all of the feelings found in the general public are present in the zoo staff as well. It is possible for an objective scientist to be humane, and zoo professionals are far from being hard hearted or cold blooded. They may not be sentimental about animals, but they have a very real love for them, and although they understand the long-term implications for species survival, individual decisions deal with animals that they know and that are in their care.

Most zoos today are grappling with the task of forming their policies on euthanasia. Not all birds eggs are set for incubation; not all mice live to grow up. The cynic may argue that only big animals such as tigers are likely to evoke a protest, that no one is disturbed by the death of a mouse or a snake. There may be truth in this, but the fact remains that euthanasia is hard to take. For a profession that is dedicated to the care and preservation of animals, the surplus problem is a hard one to handle; uniform policy is difficult to establish, and individual decisions will be far from routine. But distasteful though it may be, the need to sacrifice some younger animals to protect a species' viability will probably have to be faced. What we must understand is that if this does take place, it is an action of last resort. Any valid alternative will be accepted joyfully, and a number of such valid alternatives do exist and will be used.

In the wild, individuals from an expanding population often move away into new territory, and this is the most common solution for surplus animals in any one zoo. They go to another. Today, they can go from one zoo to another by sale or trade, loan or gift. However, they can not be sent just anywhere, for the AAZPA members have agreed not to sell animals to roadside menageries or to unqualified individuals. There are some highly qualified private breeders, especially of birds and reptiles, who are able to take

Golden lion tamarins are the best lobbiests for the cause of animal conservation. The zoo-going public adores them.

some surplus stock, but not a great number. This regulation protects animals from the appalling abuse and neglect that they might endure in badly run establishments, and it keeps them out of the hands of people who are unqualified to handle wild animals (protecting both the animal and the public) but it also narrows options.

Loan for exhibit as sterilized pairs or single sex groups effectively removes animals from the breeding population, but allows them to serve their species in other important ways. So although most inter-zoo loans are breeding loans, there are an increasing number that serve other purposes. To return to the item concerning the golden lion tamarins at the opening of this chapter, at the beginning of that breeding program in 1972, almost all of the animals in the United States were assembled in a few zoos that had space and the staff to take part in the intensive cooperative program. The other zoos loaned their animals for this purpose. Now, when there are surplus animals, these zoos can make another contribution by taking some of the non-breeders and using them as exhibits of great educational value, for the beautiful golden lion tamarin is a potent spokesman for the cause of captive propagation.

It is probable that many smaller zoos may not be actively engaged in SSPs, but they will play a very important role in these programs by offering space for what we might call "spare" animals, rather than "surplus." There is also no reason why a creature that is a poor candidate for breeding, for one reason or another, is not a good exhibit animal—and zoos are always going to need exhibits and a good many of them. This will take care of a substantial number of the spare animals.

Another possibility is to release some to universities and other accredited establishments for certain well-defined types of research. The AAZPA has strict guidelines for this. Such research must be of direct benefit to other zoo or wild animals, not biomedical research for humans. It must be humane, and might entail such things as behavioral studies or studies of animal nutrition, the means of developing new contraceptives for different species or of vaccines to fight disease. In short, things that will serve to preserve animals, both in the zoo and in the wild. Such research is very important, and better conducted with captive bred animals than those taken from the wild for that purpose.

The solution closest to everyone's heart, and the ultimate aim of captive propagation, is to return animals to the wild, to once again live free and enrich our world with their presence. Many people have considered this to be visionary, primarily because there is so little wild left for the animals to go to, though some events of recent years have changed this picture.

It is true that reintroduction can be a formidable operation. There is more to a

A young visitor who may never journey to Galapagos or Aldabra is able to meet a giant tortoise under the guidance of volunteer guide, Jo McFarlane.

successful release than opening a crate and waving farewell; in fact under those conditions, the animal, being sensible on the whole, may refuse to leave. The most obvious condition for a successful operation is that there be a part of the original habitat left that can be protected from further destruction and which contains enough food, shelter, and space for more animals. This last is important, because if others of the species still live in the area, they may not take kindly to newcomers. Animals are creatures of habit. They are often territorial; they have established routes of travel, regular feeding and watering places, well-known lairs, and established family groups. A stranger may be attacked tooth and claw or cold-shouldered out of the way.

A few years ago, a young tiger in the Ganges Delta region of India formed the habit of feeding on villager's cattle, and finally killed a village woman. Indian law now protects tigers unless they are confirmed man-eaters, and in an attempt to save this one, Dr. John Seidensticker, then a field researcher for the National Zoo, flew in from where he was working in Nepal. Seidensticker and an Indian research team darted the tiger, caged him, and moved him to a tiger reserve, where he was far from humans and where they hoped he would do no more harm. Four days after his release, they found the tiger lying dead within feet of the transport crate, covered with the tooth and claw marks of another male tiger who had resented this rival in his territory. It is often impossible to place another animal, especially a big one, in a reserve that may, in fact, already be carrying all of that species it can hold.

It is also futile to replace animals in their original setting as long as the original threat to their existence remains. Giant tortoises once roamed the Galapagos Islands in great numbers; now they are extinct on some of the islands, and very rare on most of them. Although the whalers who once captured the great creatures for food on their voyages have passed into history, their legacy, and that of other settlers, of feral cats, dogs, goats, and pigs remains, and these animals prey on tortoise eggs as well as the young tortoises.

Researchers at the Darwin Research Station meet this threat by digging up tortoise nests and bringing the eggs into the station, incubating them there, and rearing the youngsters until they are big enough to be released safely, an example of the ways in which zoos and reserves are using similar techniques to fulfill the same functions.

In separate pens at the Darwin Station, baby tortoises from the different islands stump slowly about, feeding and growing, each marked on its shell to identify it as its home island's distinct form. This kind of captive rearing is only a short-term measure, designed to increase the number of tortoises and not a solution to the tortoise's problems. Workers from the Research Station reinforce the breeding program with a campaign to wipe out the feral animals so that the tortoises and the other members of those island's incredible fauna can live in safety.

The species' own behavior may determine whether release is simple or difficult.

A yellow phase green tree python hatchling will soon take on the green coloring of its species.

Tortoises and snakes can stump or slither away from the holding box and soon blend into the landscape; most of their behavior is innate. Antelope or bison may adjust with relatively little difficulty. But many animals need to learn how to live wild. Predators, both bird and mammal, learn their hunting skills during the long dependent period they spent with their parents. Those who have read Joy Adamson's *Born Free* may remember that this is a long slow process taking great skill and patience.

Primates also learn a great many of their survival skills from life with their parents. The fifteen golden lion tamarins that were returned to Brazil were not released into the forest the day after their arrival; they went through a process of re-education that lasted for six months. They are still being closely monitored. There have been other attempts to release primates, usually young animals that have been confiscated after unauthorized captures, but there is almost no experience with adult or juvenile captive-born animals. The outcome will be watched with great interest by the zoo community.

Captive-born animals may be too tame for their own good. Although they do keep much of their wild behavior in the zoo, they still become accustomed to having humans around them and lose some of their innate fear of man. Probably those that adjust best to the zoo are those with the capacity for tameness, and some become very attached to humans. Cheetahs released in the Serengeti have continued to visit safari camps, amiably seeking human contact, and Daphne Sheldrick, the wife of the former warden of Tsavo National Park in Kenya, writes in her delightful book, *Animal Kingdom,* of her hand-reared rhino who after his release would visit the tented camp in the park. Delighted tourists started feeding him and offering him a few quick drinks in the bar tent as a nightcap, thereby undoing all the careful preparations that had been made to enable him to live as a wild rhino. All such animals have to be relocated for their own safety, as well as that of others, and sometimes have to be destroyed.

Many factors have to be considered when reintroductions are contemplated, such as the animals genetic lineage, their membership in the proper subspecies, the possibility of carrying disease into the wild population, or the captive animals' lack of resistance to diseases in the wild. One of the newly released Andean condors died from eating its natural food—carrion—because it had not had the long-term exposure required to build up a resistance to the bacteria it contained.

Reintroduction is expensive. There are costs of land acquisition, of wardens, of fences, of food while the animals become adjusted, workers to help with and monitor that adjustment, costs of transport. It has been said, jokingly, that the reintroduction of the Hawaiian goose required the services of one Ph.D. and three graduate students per goose. While this is an exaggeration, such projects are labor intensive. Ten years of work and several million dollars have gone into the reintroduction of the peregrine falcon. And it could cost half a million dollars or better to reintroduce ten tigers.

This sounds very discouraging, but it is the dark side of rescue and release. There have been reintroductions, and there will be others. Many are under way today, and each one tells us more about what is needed for a successful operation.

Perhaps the most unusual and ambitious reintroduction project is taking place in Israel, where several reserves have been set up and stocked with the animals that lived there in Biblical times. This project serves both to protect endangered species and to restore something of the Middle Eastern heritage. Avraham Yoffe, a hero of the Six Day War, and a passionate conservationist who once moved an army camp to protect a field of wildflowers, has been a moving force in this attempt.

The animals in these reserves are all mentioned in the Bible, but by names that have gone through many translations. For example, the King James Bible talks of coneys—

Persian onagers may look like donkeys, but they are a swift, hardy, wild species, now a rare one in their native central Asia.

In 1972 the National Zoo sent two scimitar-horned oryx to be released into the Haibar Reserve in Israel.

rabbits to the English translators—and the Revised Version talks of badgers in the same context, an animal unknown in Israel. These are really hyraxes, chubby little creatures that scamper among the rocks, and, incredible as it may seem, are remotely related to elephants. The first challenge was to identify which animals were really part of the original fauna.

From these species, there had to be selected those which were available and could be safely placed in the new reserves. Although lions march through the Bible with Daniel and Samson, they will not be restored to the reserves. Large predators cannot be included in reserves of this size, because they would prey too heavily on the other animals, and might move out to harry domestic livestock.

As the Haibar Arava Reserve was fenced in, the Israelis found that they had enclosed a bonus in the form of a native herd of Dorcas gazelles, known in the Bible as *Tsvi Hàmidbar,* and these became the first residents. They were joined by animals from all over the world. Asiatic wild asses, or onagers, came from the zoo at Rotterdam; scimitar-horned oryx from the National Zoo; Arabian oryx from the Los Angeles Zoo; Somali wild asses from the Catskill Game Farm.

The reserves are now established and running and appear to be a success, though they face certain difficulties inherent in small reserve management. They are not large, and additional space is hard to come by. Wild asses get into vicious mating battles and subdominant males are injured. Food runs short, and at certain seasons the wardens have to bring supplementary rations. However, most of the animals are doing well, and, in fact, many of the difficulties of the project stem from the healthy birth rate. With good and attentive management, these reserves can be a proving ground for similar ones in other such protected regions, places where a bit of a region's natural animal diversity can be preserved.

Reintroduction, by various techniques, is no longer visionary. Peregrine falcons once more fly in the skies of the eastern United States, and are breeding in the wild, the outcome of captive propagation at Cornell University. That experience, and the experience with the release of zoo-bred Andean condors, will be applied to the release of California condors. Healthy bald eagles and ospreys have been hatched in nests of adults that were sterilized by pesticide residues, often from eggs laid by captive birds. Captive-bred eaglets have been accepted by the adult birds as well, restoring healthy young birds to depleted populations. Nene, or Hawaiian, geese once more gabble softly as they feed on the slopes of the Haleakela Volcano in Hawaii, the descendants of birds bred in England at the Wildfowl Trust at Slimbridge. The success of the wisent herd in Poland encourages those who might wish to establish semi-wild herds of Père David's deer and Przewalski's horses or other such animals.

Intelligent management assures the healthy, vigorous stocks that make such things possible. It assures that Siberian tigers and Asian lions and other such large animals, probably doomed in the wild, will find sanctuary in captivity. It assures that a diversity of healthy animals will still appear in our zoos. For the millions of people who have little contact with the wild world and who may never be able to travel far to see it, this is an important consideration. How can we ever learn to value that which we never see or experience?

ONLY WHAT WE UNDERSTAND

Zoos are many things to many people. Webster's defines a zoo as a "place where wild animals are kept for public viewing." The National Zoo was founded for "the advancement of science and the education and recreation of the people." For one visitor, the zoo is a place for a family outing or a Sunday school picnic. For another, it is a place where her children can see their storybook animals in action; for still another, a place to stroll and escape the city streets. It is a survival center in some eyes, a behavioral laboratory in the perceptions of others, a center for education to a third.

Every one of those perceptions is valid. Each one is a sound reason for a zoo to exist. It may be tempting to climb out on an exclusive and scientific limb devoted to endangered species, but it is unlikely that this constitutes the whole of the public's conception of what a zoo should offer. Zoo directors must consider other important obligations. For example, most zoos rely on gate receipts for a substantial part of their support and most visitors come to the zoo in search of recreation of one sort or another. A secondary reason is usually the zoo's value in their children's education.

Critics of zoos question the value of their educational and recreational functions as a justification for the continued existence of zoos. They argue that whatever educational function a zoo can offer could be satisfied equally well by the use of some of the excellent wildlife films. They feel that there is no good reason for keeping animals in captivity for public amusement, that this is exploitative of the animals, and that today's zoos, with their spacious cages and wide lawns, are simply better-looking versions of the nineteenth-century menagerie. Although their criticism is based on their concern for animal welfare, they sometimes reinforce this with criticism of the behavior of a minority of zoo visitors. Admittedly, there are days when blaring radios and screaming children make it seem that these critics have a point, but such visitors are the exception.

While every zoo has its compliment of the rowdy and the raucous, who feed the elephants inedible objects and toss paper cups at the seals, they are far outnumbered by those who truly enjoy the experience and go away refreshed. One visitor confessed to a guide at the Bird House, "I really can't tell one bird from another, and I'm afraid that I

Secure on its father's back, a young Barbary macaque looks dreamy and contented.

The beauty and serenity of these eider ducks offer visitors refreshment of the spirit.

don't care. I just come here to watch them because they are so beautiful." If we consider recreation to be "refreshment of body or mind" (as does Webster's Dictionary), this sort of contact is a tremendously important recreational resource.

Traditionally, the zoo is a nice place to take the kids on Sunday, not from any urge to learn more about animal behavior or the wilder flights of the taxonomists, but to spend some time in a place where there are green lawns and tall trees, where graceful animals lie peacefully chewing their cuds, where colorful birds flutter in tropical settings, where sea lions plunge and cavort in cool water. Even when the crowds are thick, such scenes are far removed from the urban—or even suburban—setting and, possibly more important, this is the *only* contact that much of our population has with the animal world. Today few children have the chance to visit grandfather on his farm because grandfather lives in the city too, if not in a Florida condominium.

Contact with animals is important. Not only is it difficult to ever fully appreciate the

184

reality of an animal from the sterile medium of film, no matter how excellent, but psychologists now tell us that contact with living animals affects our well-being. Such experiences can accomplish everything from lowering our blood pressure to releasing our emotions. A tank of tropical fish can lower the tension of the dentist's waiting room. A dog can effect an emotional release for even the most uptight of executives. After all, we humans evolved in the company of other animals, became hunters, where knowledge of the ways of the prey were essential to survival, and graduated to herdsmen, where concern for other creatures was a way of life. Only in the last hundred years have we moved away from our fellows, so it is hardly surprising to learn that the need for such contact still lurks somewhere in our being. It may be that we ignore this at our peril.

Exposure to animals in a good zoo may lay the foundation for a real love affair with the animal kingdom, for once the visitor is there, he is open to the influence of some of the world's best educators, the animals themselves. With their beauty, their potential for excitement, and their moments of humor, animals are excellent spokesmen for their own cause. Dr. Theodore Reed, the former Director of the National Zoo, says that the animals in the zoo are there as ambassadors for their kind in the wild. Part of any

Sarus cranes tending their chicks endear themselves to the public and call attention to the status of wild cranes.

ambassador's mission is to make a favorable presentation to the world of the needs and interests of those that he represents. Zoos have a tremendous potential for education through these ambassadors, allowing them to gain public interest and sympathy and then emphasizing their plight.

Not long ago, there was a morning when the trumpeting of an angry African elephant could be heard throughout the zoo. The white rhinos had just come out into their yard, which was next door to that of the African elephant, and their appearance had apparently disturbed her morning meditations. It is risky to attribute human feelings to animals, but it did seem that our elephant was irked by those big beasts next door. She trumpeted, she stamped, she flapped her big ears, and loped up and down the edge of the moat that divided her from the rhinos. It was an impressive sight for, until you see an elephant on the move, it is hard to imagine the speed and silence of the great animal's movements.

To make matters worse, the rhinos paid no attention to this pachyderm tantrum, but continued to root and roll in their mud wallow. Finally, tried beyond endurance, the elephant scooped up a rock about the size of a grapefruit in her trunk, and with a neat underhand delivery, pitched it at the rhinos. The rock fell short, but the action must have soothed her feelings and satisfied her honor, but she ambled off to scratch her back against a post.

It would have been hard for anyone to watch this and not come away with a fresh perception of elephants, some impression of the intelligence and individuality that makes them such wonderful beasts. One little girl summed it up by saying, "No one should kill elephants. Elephants are more precious than ivory."

The importance of education in the zoo is recognized by the AAZPA and is an integral part of the Species Survival Plans. But most zoos have not yet realized their full potential in this area, probably in part because the information that they might offer is so rich and so diverse. And what is more, the zoo audience is a very diverse assembly, so that information that fascinates one visitor may turn another off. (One zoo guide, talking with a group of children who showed every sign of interest, was more than a little disconcerted to hear one chaperoning mother say to another, "Bo-o-o-r-ing!") Finally, it is very easy to become simplistic when discussing conservation, and many professionals shy away from doing so in brief. Nevertheless, many in the profession feel that the zoo's contribution to conservation through education may be as important as the contribution made through captive breeding. A Senegalese writer, Baba Dioum, sums up this line of thought when he says:

The African elephant stamped back and forth, waving her trunk and flapping her big ears.

River otters at play, under water, and on the surface.

In the end, we will conserve only what we love.
We will love only what we understand.
We will understand only what we have been taught.

Although there are a number of other methods, exhibit labels are the traditional way to communicate with the public. But what should these say? Should they tell where an animal is from or what it eats, its age or its species' status in the wild, or the details of its social life or interesting anecdotes? A visitor might ask any of these questions and all might be considered pertinent, but, short of placing something the size of a billboard by each exhibit, choices have to be made.

The result of these conflicts is that many zoo educators live the lives of frustrated Ancient Mariners, longing to buttonhole passing visitors and share with them the wonders of the animal world, but restrained by the visitor's undoubted right to acquire information in his own way. It might be easier if all visitors could be counted upon for the degree of sensitivity that Dr. Louis Thomas showed when he unexpectedly encountered, at the Tuscon Zoo, a tank of otters and a tank of beavers. In his book, *The Medusa and the Snail,* he tells of the encounter:

> Within just a few feet of your face, on either side, beavers and otters are at play, under water and on the surface, swimming toward your face and then away, more filled with life than any creatures I have seen before in all my days. Except for the glass, you could reach out and touch them.
>
> I was transfixed. As I now recall it, there was only one sensation in my head: pure elation mixed with amazement at such perfection. Swept off my feet, I floated from one side to the other, swiveling my brain, staring astounded at the beavers, then at the otters. I could hear shouts across my corpus callosum, from one hemisphere to the other. I remember thinking with what was left of my consciousness, that I wanted no part of the science of beavers and otters; I

Just watching the fascinating behavior of the prairie dogs might start a life-long love affair with the Animal Kingdom.

wanted never to know how they performed their marvels; I wished for no news about the physiology of their breathing, the coordination of their muscles, their vision, their endocrine systems, their digestive tracts. I hoped never to have to think of them as collections of cells. All I asked for was the full hairy complexity then before my eyes, of whole, intact beavers and otters in motion.

If one animal in each zoo could reach out to each single visitor in this way, we might need no other educational programs. Still, Thomas's experience notwithstanding, there is much of interest and importance in the study of animal behavior, in dispelling myths and growing to a deeper appreciation of their intelligence. Conservation efforts are often hampered by popular images of animals as good guys and bad guys, stereotypes of little people in furry suits, turtles that can unbutton their shells, slimy snakes and ravenous wolves. We will never preserve the wolf or the tiger or any other creature by cheering it or condemning it; only by seeing it as a hard-working member of a community, with its own set of needs, habits, and perceptions. We must learn to invest other creatures with the dignity that comes from understanding.

One group of children, visiting the zoo with their teacher, stopped to watch a family of Barbary macaques who were busy with that monkey occupation known as grooming. The teacher had explained that this was not solely a matter of "looking for fleas," as it is often called, although a monkey would remove a flea if it came across one. Instead, grooming is a ritual with rather set rules about who grooms whom and when. It does clean the groomee's fur (and seems to feel wonderful) and rewards the groomer with tiny flakes of salt from the skin, but it is very important for its effect on the group's social structure, helping to cement social bonds.

The children had absorbed this and were watching a particularly intent grooming group with interest and some amusement. A big male macaque lay stretched on his side with a blissful expression on his freckled face, while a female, earnestly and with great concentration, parted his fur; her baby reached out a tentative paw in imitation when it was sure it would be safe. It was a very relaxed and rather charming scene.

As they were watching, a trio of teenagers came along and stopped to snicker and made rude comments. One of the schoolchildren turned to his teacher and asked why those big kids were laughing. Unwilling to say, frankly, "Because they're a bunch of oafs," the teacher shrugged and answered, "I suppose they must think it looks funny." The little boy warmed his teacher's heart by looking at the jeerers thoughtfully and saying, "But it isn't that kind of funny when you know why they do it."

Why they do it. This forms another part of the educational effort in zoos. In accordance with their resources, which are necessarily varied, zoos are engaged in the

Grooming is an important part of monkey and ape social life. A female Barbury macaque concentrates on her infant.

more advanced study of animal behavior. They offer students opportunities to study animals under conditions that are more natural than those of the laboratory, and they offer the only opportunity to observe things that are impossible to follow in the wild, such as long-term studies of how animals avoid inbreeding, which take a number of years and require accurate knowledge of relationships. Many zoos have university affiliations, supplying faculty, providing students with a place to observe animals, and serving as teaching centers.

In the zoo, research in veterinary medicine goes forward, usually with benefits to exotic animals in the wild and in zoos, occasionally with benefits to humans. A gorilla with arthritis has been of great interest to medical doctors. Research into nutrition of

The development of a young orangutan is interesting to students of both animal and human behavior.

As a part of a study of native Virginia wildlife, junior assistant Greg Sanders places a radio transmitter collar on a tranquilized bobcat with the help of volunteer Dottie Emerick.

exotic animals has provided us with results in longer-lived, healthier animals. Zoo keepers travel between institutions, learning and teaching new techniques in husbandry. Scientists go out from the zoo world to work in the field, in China with pandas, in South America with tamarins and jaguars, with elephants in Sri Lanka, and with people everywhere. They carry new equipment and techniques, act as advisors, sharing information and skills.

In one such training project, the National Zoo makes use of the Conservation and Research Center at Front Royal, both to study the problems associated with small, isolated reserves, and to train wildlife managers and biologists from the United States and the developing nations. With its three thousand acres of forests and fields, the Center is larger than some one hundred of the world's parks and reserves, and the native wildlife there, and in the adjoining Shenandoah National Park, face the same problems. Using raccoons, opossums, bobcats, and other residents, the staff at the Center and from the Zoo study the comings and goings of this small community, using these to devise plans for similar tracts around the globe.

Students come here to learn more about captive propagation and wildlife management. One prospective student wrote that his game department was attempting to capture orangutans and relocate them before their forests were destroyed, but the only methods that he had of capturing the apes was to drive them into a tree, cut the surrounding trees, and then grease the trunk and wait for the ape to slide down. Confining apes to trees and then cutting the tree is a traditional practice, but he hoped to discover a more effective method. Undoubtedly he did, because live trapping and radio tracking techniques are among the things that students learn.

Education and training spread from such centers may be another great contribution that zoos make to conservation. While captive breeding is important and, eventually, essential for the survival of a number of species of large animals, its lessons may prove more important than its achievements. The zoo ark can only hold a few of the hundreds of thousands of living things that share the earth; the others must be saved within their own habitats. Dr. John Seidensticker, assistant curator at the National Zoo's Department of Zooligical Research, says, "It is from the zoo experience rather than from the study of large natural ecosystems that the expertise will be developed to address the critical conditions in the planning of smaller reserves, for reintroducing species that have been lost from natural areas, and for correcting faunal imbalances and other disruptions which plague small, recovering, and/or insular habitats."

For, what is really a zoo? In the March 1983 issue of the magazine, *National Geographic,* writer and naturalist Douglas H. Chadwick tells about the Etosha National Park in Namibia. Etosha is one of the largest parks in the world, a great wildlife sanctuary where, if anywhere, surrounded by five hundred miles of eight-foot fence, one would think that the native animals could live their lives undisturbed. But resident animals are moved out of the park while others of their species are brought in to effect genetic exchanges. One section of the park is set aside for intensive propagation of endangered species. And even this vast park is becoming overcrowded; surplus animals are becoming a problem as they destroy their own habitat. Some lionesses already carry contraceptive implants, and some culling will soon have to be done. In its season, thousands of foreign visitors come to see the animal spectacle. Zoo or park, park or zoo, the distinctions are fine.

Any discussion of captive propagation and the management of wild populations raises certain ethical questions. Preventing extinction carries certain costs—in terms of animals' lives, in terms of impacts on human populations, and in terms of money. Are we willing to accept the idea that the preservation of diversity justifies the use of a

We must decide how far we can go in allocating scarce resources of money and land to the survival of the black rhinoceros.

limited resource—land—for this purpose? Can we justify the use of artificial insemination, with its associated medical manipulations, or the juggling of animal's social lives? Can we justify the use of possibly billions of dollars for this purpose? Is not extinction the natural fate of all species, including our own?

To address this last question first, it is true that all species do eventually become extinct, though a great many go on for millions of years before they meet their end. There are many reasons advanced for this, but the usual reason for large numbers of extinctions within a certain period, such as that which saw the fall of the dinosaurs, is a drastic change in the conditions of the life that then prevailed. In any case, such changes leave a species no time to muster its genetic resources and adapt to the change.

Competition is another cause of extinction, as a prolific, adaptable species appropriates the living space and resources of another. In both senses, we humans are responsible for the extinctions taking place today. A random flip of the evolutionary deck has tossed up our prolific, adaptable species, and we have profoundly altered the face of the earth in the last 400 years. Some may argue that this is our right, and that extinction is the inevitable fate of species that cannot adapt, but this smacks of saying that their extinction is their own fault. Tamarins should learn to fly to another forest or to live in burrows and rhinos should learn to shoot back.

Ours is supposedly a rational species, capable of using good sense, capable of seeing the results of our actions, and taking steps to modify these results. We are not a massive, unknowing force, a glacier or a volcano, nor always an uncaring one. In fact, we have rare moments of showing altruistic behavior of a high order, reaching out to other peoples, and now to other species. And because of this, because we have understanding and the ability to act at a time when action is imperative, we will not be able to plead ignorance when our actions are judged at the bar of the future.

What will be the charges of that tribunal? What value has a species to justify the costs of saving it? Many reasons have been advanced for the preservation of diversity,

For all its importance to the future of its species, a baby animal remains a thing of wonder, a heart-warming sight that carries its own message.

but one of the most compelling may be that we do not know what that value is. A number of good economic arguments are offered; the great importance of many plants and their products in our economy and the probable presence of others of their ilk, the possible use of such animals as antelope and some rodents to increase the world's food supply, the value of certain animals to medical research. Most of these economic uses are valid, but they could be met from other sources today. The future is another story. We do not know what our descendants may need. A food source that is today unacceptable or economically impossible to exploit may become of great importance. Plants of medicinal value are undoubtedly lying hidden in the rain forest. It is only recently that the armadillo was recognized as a good animal model for the study of leprosy.

We do not know what species may be central to the workings of certain ecosystems. Certainly not all hold such positions, but in many cases, we have not the faintest idea which ones are expendable. We are far from clear about the workings of rain forests as systems, how they affect climate locally or worldwide. We are very much like children busily engaged in dismantling a complex machine without the faintest idea of what its purpose might be, and certainly without any ability to put it back together again. Philosophers may argue about how much we owe to future generations, but a world that is still in working order, with its options still in place, would appear to be a minimum obligation.

Species diversity is important for more than economic reasons. Our species is a restless, inquisitive, creative kind of animal, and the existence of other forms of plants and animals adds to the color and challenge and diversity of life. Many of us will never go to Africa to see the great herds, or to the Bering Sea to see the thousands of sea birds clustered on the cliffs or to the Amazon to see caymans lying on the sand bars or hear parrots shouting overhead. But, for a moment, picture a world where no one could do so, for these no longer existed. A golden lion tamarin may not be of great importance in the greater scheme of things, but the forest would be a drabber place without the flash of that little golden body.

In recent years, various people and organizations have spent millions to move the Temples of Abu Simbel above the waters of the Aswan Dam. Funds and volunteers from all over the world flowed into Florence to help save its art treasures after the Arno flooded. Millions are spent restoring old buildings, sometimes of very questionable historic value. Surely, living plants and animals have as much value to humanity as any of these. It seems egocentric to value the works of our own hands, no matter how wonderful, above those that share with us the gift of life.

Once a species is gone, it is gone for all time. We can well argue that there is little enough beauty in the world, and increasingly little enough diversity, without the destruction of more. Should anyone object to the sort of management that is needed to preserve this beauty, they might ask themselves if their children or grandchildren will feel the same. The actions and decisions that we make today had better be made with wisdom and foresight, for they will determine how diverse the future will be, how much beauty, how many options the world will retain.

In spite of its changing role, a good zoo is much more than an earnest scientific effort. It is a lively and living museum, a place in which to watch and to wonder and to laugh. A trio of zebras buck and wheel, engaging in mock battle with flying hoofs. A tiny gazelle calf pokes its big eyes and blunt nose above the long grass, gazing at a new world. Red kangaroos lie in abandoned poses, basking in the sunshine. An elephant, her mind seemingly on higher things, reaches her trunk through the railings to snatch her keeper's broom. A kit fox pokes his nose from his den, big ears pricked, whiskers twitching. Perhaps he can smell the prairie dogs that bustle about the mouth of their tunnel nearby. Flamingos honk and fuss, feathers ruffled so that they look like so many long-stemmed pink chrysanthemums. All are alert and healthy, and, so far as anyone can arrange it, doing their own thing.

SPECIES INDEX

Photographs that have received different degrees of enlargement can give a false impression of animal's relative sizes. Here, together with their natural range and scientific names, are the pertinent dimensions of these creatures. Measurements are given in terms of the way animals are most often viewed: horses are measured at the shoulder, but an otter from nose to tail; a bird from beak to tail (or occasionally wing tip to wing tip) and a snake by length. Sometimes male and female differ so much in size that it is necessary to give measurements for both.

Ass, Somali Wild, *Equus asinus somalicus.* Range: Ethiopia, Somalia; Height: 43 inches; Weight: 414 pounds; Status: Endangered.

Bandicoot, Brindled, *Isoodon macrourus.* Range: Northern Australia and New Guinea; Length: 9–19 inches; Tail: 11 inches; Weight: 3 pounds.

Bison, American, *Bison bison.* Range: Plains of western United States; Height: 5–6 feet; Weight: 1000–2000 pounds; Status: Stable with protection.

Bison, European (Wisent), *Bison bonasus.* Range: Forests of eastern Poland and western Soviet Union; Height: 5–6 feet; Weight: 1000–2000 pounds; Status: Stable with protection.

Boa, Emerald Tree, *Corallus canina.* Range: Tropical forests of South America; Length: to 4 feet.

Bowerbird, Satin, *Ptilonorhynchus violaceus.* Eastern Australia; Length: 13 inches.

Bullfrog, African, *Pyxicephalus adspersa.* Range: Southern Africa; Length: 4–6 inches.

Cassowary, Double wattled, *Casuarius casuarius.* Range: Northern Australia and New Guinea; Height: 65 inches.

Camel, Bactrian, *Camelus bactrianus.* Range: Central Asia; Height: 7 feet.

Cheetah, *Acinonyx jubatus.* Range: Africa, from Sudan to Union of South Africa; Height: 31 inches; Weight: 126–143 pounds; Status: Endangered.

Chimpanzee, *Pan troglodites.* Range: Central Africa; Body length: 27 inches (F)–36 inches (M); Stands: 3½–5 feet; Weight: 90–110 pounds.

Condor, Andean, *Vultur gryphus.* Range: Andes, from Venezuela to Straits of Magellan; Wing span: 10 feet; Weight: 20–25 pounds; Status: Endangered.

Condor, California, *Gymnogryps californianus.* Range: Coast ranges of California; Wing span: 10 feet; Weight: 20–25 pounds; Status: On the verge of extinction.

Crane, Sandhill, *Grus canadensis.* Range: Northwestern and southeastern North America; Height: 42 inches; Weight: 10 pounds; Status: Cuban, Greater, and Florida subspecies are endangered.

Crane, Sarus, *Grus Antigone.* Range: India, Burma, Thailand; Height: 60 inches.

Crocodile, Cuban, *Crocodylus rhombifer.* Range: Zapata and Lanier Swamps of Cuba; Length: 7–8 feet (F), 8–9 feet (M). Status: Endangered.

Deer, Pere David's, *Elaphurus davidianus.* Range: Formerly northern China; Height: 45 inches; Weight: 300 pounds; Status: Extinct in the wild.

Dik dik, Kirk's, *Madogua kirkii.* Range: Kenya and Tanzania; Height: 16 inches; Weight: 12 pounds.

Dog, African Wild, *Lycaon pictus*. Range: Sub-Saharan Africa; Height: 24 inches; Weight: 40 pounds (F)–60 pounds (M); Status: Declining.

Dog, Bush, *Speothos venaticus*. Range: Panama to Paraguay east of the Andes; Length: 22½–29½ inches; Tail: 5–6 inches; Weight: 11–15 pounds.

Eagle, American Bald, *Haliaeetus leucocephalus*. Range: Gulf of Mexico to Arctic; Length: 34 inches; Status: Endangered in eastern United States, stable in Alaska.

Elephant, African, *Loxodonta africana*. Range: Africa south of the Sahara; Height: 8–10 feet; Weight: 4–6 tons. Status: Threatened.

Fennec, *Fennecus zerda*. Range: North Africa to Arabia; Length: 14–16 inches; Tail: 7–12 inches; Weight: 3.3 pounds.

Flamingo, Greater, *Phoenicopterus ruber*. Range: West Indes, South America; Height: 45–50 inches.

Frog, Horned, *Ceratophrys ornata*. Range: Argentina; Length; 4½ inches.

Frog, Red-eyed Tree, *Agalychnis callidryas*. Range: Central America; Length: 1 inch.

Gaur, *Bibos gaurus*. Range: Northern India; Height: 6–7 feet; Weight: 1500 pounds; Status: Endangered.

Gazelle, Dama, *Gazella dama*. Range: Chad, Somalia, Ethiopia; Height: 35–43 inches; Weight: 160 pounds; Status: Endangered.

Gazelle, Dorcas, *Gazella dorcas*. Range: North Africa into Israel; Height: 22–26 inches; Weight: 45–50 pounds; Status: Endangered.

Gazelle, Speke's, *Gazella spekes*. Range: Ethiopia and Somalia; Height: 24 inches; Weight: 40 pounds; Status: Endangered.

Gibbon, White-cheeked, *Hylobates concolor*. Range: Southeast Asia; Body length: 18–25 inches; Weight: 9–15 pounds.

Giraffe, *Giraffa camelopardalis*. Range: Eastern and southern Africa south of the Sahara; Height: 18 feet (M); Weight: 1½ tons.

Goose, Nene, *Branta sandvicensis*. Range: Islands of Hawaii and Maui; Length: 23–28 inches; Status: Endangered.

Goose, Red-breasted, *Branta ruficolis*. Range: Siberia to Caspian Sea; Length: 22 inches.

Gorilla, Lowland, *Gorilla gorilla*. Range: Forests of Equitorial Africa; Body length: 39–42 inches; Stands: 6 feet (M); Weight: 165 pounds (F) to 300–400 pounds (M); Status: Threatened.

Horse, Przewalski's or **Mongolian Wild,** *Equus przewalskii*. Range: Mongolia; Height: 3½–4 feet; 800 pounds; Status: Probably extinct in the wild.

Hyrax, Rock, *Heterohyrax syriacus*. Range: Middle East to Southwest Africa; Length: 12–15 inches; Weight: 8 pounds.

Jaguar, *Panthera onca*. Range: Southeast United States to Brazil; Body length: 5–6 feet; Tail: 25–36 inches; Weight: 150–275 pounds; Status: Endangered.

Kangaroo, Red, *Megaleia rufa*. Range: Inland plains of Australia; Body length: 31–40 inches; Tail: 27–38 inches; Weight: 66 pounds.

Lapwing, Yellow-wattled, *Lobipluvia malabarica*. Malabar Coast of India; Length: 12 inches.

Lemur, Ruffed, *Varecia varigatus*. Range: Rain forest of east coast of Madagascar; Length: 24 inches; Tail: 24 inches; Weight: 6.6 pounds; Status: Endangered.

Leopard, *Panthera pardus*. Range: Africa through the Middle East to Asia; Length: 36–59 inches; Weight: 200 pounds.

Lion, *Panthera leo*. Range: Africa south of the Sahara; Length: 6–7½ feet; Tail: 3 feet; Height: 3 feet; Weight: 385–500 pounds.

Lion, Asian, *Panthera leo persica*. Range: Found only in the Gir Forest of western India; Status: Endangered.

Macaque, Barbary, *Macaca sylvana*. Range: Morocco, Algeria, Gibraltar; Length: 24 inches (no tail); Weight: 24 pounds.

Macaque, Lion-Tailed, *Macaca silenus*. Range: Western Ghat Range of India; Length: 18–24 inches; Tail: 10–15 inches; Weight: 14 pounds; Status: Endangered.

Mallard, *Anas platyrhynchos*. Range: Breeds western North America east into New England, winters Atlantic and Gulf coast; Length: 20–28 inches.

Meercat, *Suricata suricatta*. Range: Southern Africa; Length: 9¾–13¾ inches; Tail: 6½–9½ inches; Weight: 1.3–1.7 pounds.

Mongoose, Dwarf, *Helogale parvula*. Range: Africa-Ethiopia to the Orange River; Length: 8–9 inches; Tail: 5 inches; Weight: 20 ounces.

Monkay, Colobus, *Colobus quereza*. Range: Senegal, Ethiopia, Kenya, Uganda; Length: 22–24 inches; Tail: 30–32 inches; Weight: 9–11 pounds; Status: Endangered.

Mynah, Rothschild's, *Leucospar rothschildi*. Range: Island of Bali; Length: 8 inches; Status: Endangered.

Okapi, *Okapia johnstoni*. Range: Rain forest of Zaire; Height: 54 inches; Weight: 450 pounds; Status: Endangered.

Onager, Persian, *Equus hemionus onager*. Range: Northeastern Iran, northwestern Afganistan; Height: 4–5 feet; Weight: 570 pounds; Status: Endangered.

Oryx, Scimitar-horned, *Oryx tao*. Range: Southern edge of Sahara from Mauritania to the Red Sea; Height: 4 feet; Weight: 450 pounds; Status: Endangered.

Orangutan, *Pongo pygmaeus*. Range: Sumatra and Borneo; Body length: 30–38 inches (Stands 3½ feet (F)–4½ feet (M); Weight: 75–100 pounds (F) to 200 pounds (M); Status: Endangered.

Otter, River, *Lutra canadensis*. Range: North American from tree line to Florida except southwestern United States and southern California; Length: 34–57 inches; Weight: 10–30 pounds.

Owl, Snowy, *Nyctea scandiaca*. Range: Circumpolar in Arctic and sub-Artic; Length: 20–26 inches.

Panda, Giant, *Ailuropoda melanoleuca*. Range: Mountains of western Szechwan, China; Length: 4–6 feet; Weight: 250–300 pounds; Status: Endangered.

Panda, Red, *Ailurus fulgens*. Range: Nepal, Sikkim, Yunan; Length: 20–25 inches; Tail: 11–18 inches; Weight: 7–10 pounds.

Pigeon, Crowned, *Goura cristata*. Range: New Guinea; Length: 33 inches.

Pigeon, Passenger, *Ectopistes migratorius*. Range: Central and eastern North America; Length: 17 inches; Status: Extinct.

Pintail, Northern, *Anas acuta*. Range: Breeds western North America, east to Pennsylvania; winters to Long Island and Gulf coasts; Length: 26–30 inches.

Pochard, European, *Netta rufina*. Range: Eastern Europe and Asia to Mediterranian, India and Burma; Length: 18–22 inches.

Prairie Dog, *Cynomys ludovicianus*. Range: United States and Canada in the Great Plains; Length: 12–16 inches; Weight: 2 pounds.

Python, Burmese, *Python molurus*. Range: Southeast Asia; Length: to 19 feet; Weight: to 200 pounds.

Python, Green Tree, *Chrondropython viridis*. Range: New Guinea; Length: 7 feet.

Rattlesnake, Timber, *Crotalus horridus*. Range: Minnesota to Southwest Maine, Florida, and Texas; Length: 3–6 feet.

Rhinoceros, Black, *Diceros bicornis*. Range: Ethiopia to Cape Province; Height: 4 feet 9 inches to 5 feet 6 inches; Weight: 1½–2 tons; Status: Endangered.

Rhinoceros, Indian, *Rhinoceros unicornis*. Range: Himalayan foothills of India and Nepal to Burma; Height: 6 feet; Weight: 2 tons; Status: Endangered.

Rhinoceros, Javan, *Rhinoceros sondaicus*. Range: Java; Height: 5½ feet; Weight: 1–2 tons; Status: Endangered.

Rhinoceros, Sumatran, *Didermocerus sumatrensis*. Range: Southeast Asia, Borneo, and Sumatra; Height: 4½ feet; Weight: 1 ton; Status: Endangered.

Rhinoceros, White, *Ceratotherium simum*. Range: Sudan to Zaire, Zimbabwe to southwest Africa; Height: 6 feet 6 inches; Weight: 3–4 tons; Status: Northern sub-species: endangered; Southern sub-species: stable.

Shrew, Rufous Elephant, *Elephantulus rufescens*. Length: 5¾ inches; Tail: 5¾ inches; Weight: 2 ounces.

Shrew, Tree, *Tupaia belangeri*. Range: Thailand; Length: 6–9 inches; Tail: 5½–9 inches; Weight: 5 ounces.

Snake, Rat, *Elaphe obsoleta*. Range: Eastern United States; Length: 2–8 feet.

Swan, Black, *Chenopis atratus.* Range: Australia and Tasmania; Length: 56–60 inches.

Tamarin, Golden Lion, *Leontopithecus rosalia rosalia.* Range: Coastal forest of eastern Brazil; Length: 8–13 inches; Tail: 9–15 inches; Weight: 12–24 ounces; Status: Endangered.

Teal, Blue winged, *Anas discors.* Range: Canada to South America; Length: 15–16 inches.

Tenrec, Striped, *Hemicentetes semispinosus.* Range: Madagascar; Length: 5½–6¾ inches; Weight: 4½–9½ ounces.

Tern, Inca, *Larosterna inca.* Range: Coast of Peru and Chile; Length: 16 inches.

Tiger, *Panthera tigris.* Range: Siberia to Java, Iran to China; Length: 6–9 feet; Tail: 3 feet; Weight: 220–500 pounds; Status: Endangered.

Titmouse, Tufted, *Parus bicolor.* Range: Eastern United States; Length: 6–6½ inches.

Toad, Oriental Firebellied, *Bombina orientalis.* Range: China and Korea; Length: ¾–1 inch.

Tortoise, Galapagos, *Geochelone elephantopus.* Range: Galapagos Islands; Length: 4 feet; Weight: 500 pounds; Status: Endangered.

Turkey, Wild, *Meleagris gallapayo.* Range: Southeastern United States to Mexico; Length: 48 inches.

Wolf, Timber, *Canis lupus.* Range: Alaska, Canada, Minnesota, Isle Royale in Michigan; Height: 38 inches; Weight: 60–150 pounds; Status: Endangered or extinct in all lower 48 states, except threatened in Minnesota.

Zebra, Common or **Burchell's,** *Equus burchelli.* Range: Grasslands from Kenya to northern South Africa; Height: 50–55 inches; Weight: 500–700 pounds.

Zebra, Grevy's, *Equus grevyi.* Range: Ethiopia and Somalia to northern Kenya; Height: 60 inches; Weight: 780–950 pounds; Status: Endangered.

SPECIES INCLUDED IN
SPECIES SURVIVAL PLANS
APRIL 1984

Alligator, Chinese
Barasingha
Boa, Madagascan Ground
Cheetah
Crane, White Naped
Elephants, African and Asian
Gaur
Gorilla
Horse, Asian Wild (Przewalski's)
Lemurs (Ruffed/Black)
Leopard, Snow
Lion, Asian
Macaque, Lion-tailed
Monkey, Proboscis
Mynah, Bali
Okapi
Orangutans
Oryx, Arabian

Oryx, Scimitar-horned
Otters (Asian Small-clawed and others)
Panda, Red
Penguins (Humbolt's)
Rattlesnake, Aruba Island
Rhino, Black
Rhino, Indian
Rhino, Sumatran
Rhino, White
Tapirs
Tamarin, Golden Lion
Tigers, Siberian and Javan
Toad, Puerto Rican Crested
Tortoise, Radiated
Wolf, Maned
Wolf, Red
Zebra, Grevy's

Credits

The illustrations in this book, noted by page number, are used with the express permission of the sources listed.

11, 17, 40, 45, 55, 59, 63, 83, 124, 130, 137, 139, 179, 189. Milton Tierney, Captive Wildlife Photography.

73. Zoological Society of San Diego.

103. Friends of National Zoo.

193. Fionna Sunquist.

ALL OTHER PHOTOGRAPHS. Jessie Cohen, Office of Graphics and Exhibits, National Zoological Park, Smithsonian Institution.

INDEX